The purchase of this book

was made possible

by a generous grant from

The Auen Foundation.

# ARE YOU ANYBODY?

# ARE YOU ANYBODY?

a memoir

JEFFREY TAMBOR

ILLUSTRATIONS BY BEN BARNES

RANDOM HOUSE
LARGE PRINT

Grateful acknowledgment is made to Alan Zweibel and
Garry Shandling (lyrics) and Joey Carbone (music) for
permission to use the lyrics of "It's Garry Shandling's Show,"
the theme to the show of the same name, on pages 282–283.

**Illustrations by Ben Barnes**
**Cover design by Christopher Brand**
**Cover photograph by Maarten de Boer / Getty**
**Additional photography credits can be found on
pages 353–354.**

The Library of Congress has established a
Cataloging-in-Publication record for this title.

ISBN: 978-1-5247-5562-1

www.randomhouse.com/largeprint

FIRST LARGE PRINT EDITION

Printed in the United States of America

10  9  8  7  6  5  4  3  2  1

This Large Print edition published in accord with
the standards of the N.A.V.H.

To Kasia . . . you raise me up.

# CONTENTS

It's going to happen for you,
but it's going to happen very, very late.

—JAMES BARTON HILL READING JEFFREY TAMBOR'S
PALM, WAYNE STATE UNIVERSITY, 1969

Our job in this lifetime is not to shape ourselves
into some ideal we imagine we ought to be,
but to find out who we really are and become it.

—STEVEN PRESSFIELD, THE WAR OF ART

Mr. Joseph Veltre
The Gersh Agency
New York, NY

Dear Joe,

I got a call from a Tricia Bocowski (sp?) at some publishing house. Apparently, someone on her staff was at my lecture in Boston and thought—are you sitting down?—I should write a book. She knew about Skylight Books in Los Angeles, too. Maybe she thinks my co-owning a bookstore qualifies me to write one?

Love,
Jeffrey

Ms. Joanna Burstein
The Burstein Company
Pacific Palisades, CA

Dear Joannie,

Yes, I know, but as I told Joe, let's send Tricia a kind note and tell her thank you for the books she sent— a truckload arrived last week, all memoirs and biographies. I think she's trying to tell me any asshole can write one of these—but no thanks. I love to read them, but writing them, that's for the pros.

Love and lunch,
Jeffrey

Mr. Joseph Veltre
The Gersh Agency
New York, NY

Dear Joe,

I think a meeting is a waste of everyone's time. I have four little ones at home from eleven years down to six-year-old twins. I have no time, not even for sex.

But just for shits and giggles, how much do people make writing these things?

Yes to lunch. Anytime.

Love,
Blossom

P.S. Another shipment of books arrived. It's getting a little much.

Ms. Tricia Boczkowski
Crown Archetype
New York, NY

Dear Trish,

Thank you for all the books. The third box was really unexpected.

I too enjoyed our meeting. I am so excited Jill Soloway is writing a book for you. But Jill is an accomplished writer.

The following is a short list of what I am:
1. Actor
2. Husband
3. Daddy
4. Grandparent
5. Lecturer
6. Bookstore co-owner

Short list of what I am not:
1. Writer

My wife is Polish, too.

With love,
Jeffrey

Ms. Leslie Siebert
The Gersh Agency
Los Angeles, CA

Leslie,

I know you've been out of the loop, but the people at Crown are at me to write a memoir. Part of the problem in writing such a thing is that, along with lifetime achievement awards, it makes one feel the end is drawing near.

Someone at Dunkin' Donuts the other day asked me if I was still acting. When I told them about **Transparent,** they told me they hadn't watched it but love **Curb Your Enthusiasm.**

None of this gives me much impetus to sit down and write.

Thoughts?

Love,
Blossom

Mr. Joseph Veltre
The Gersh Agency
New York, NY
**URGENT**

Dear Joe,

Now listen. I have no room for the boxes of books they keep sending. You know I have a huge hard-on for anything having to do with literature, but this is getting weird. I've donated them to the Lewisboro library for their fair coming up next month.

   Joe, I want to be very clear: I don't want these people near me.

Love,
Blossom

Dear Molly,

Keep an eye out. I'm sending you a shitload of books. Don't even ask, just start reading or donate them to the New York Public Library.

There are a lot of memoirs. Frank Langella's book is fun and inventive and short. John Cleese is daunting and as thick as a telephone book—and apparently it's only Part I. The fella from the Rolling Stones, although I don't know the music, I love his candor. Did he have help? Lithgow always comes through, and Bruce—Bruuuuuuce! (advance reader's copy)—very thoughtful and moving. Also telephone-book size.

All of these were to give me insight and courage to write. Then I read Tina Fey. It and she are perfection. I vowed never to write a word.

Enjoy the shipment.

Love,
Dad

Dear Todd,

Thanks for your call. I never check my home line, ever, so I fear this message is way, way late and I'm verging on rude. I'm sorry I hurt your feelings. I'm so sorry, I can't have coffee with you. But you see I don't live in Los Angeles anymore, haven't for four years now. We are in northern Westchester, "upstate."

I am writing a book for Crown and my coffee days are few and far between, except for the thousands of cups I have been making with my Keurig. Have you tried Dunkin' Donuts Dark Roast? Yummy, and one cup is equivalent to twenty direct slaps across the face.

I'm sitting in a coffee shop "upstate" as I type this. It's ten o'clock, and I'm the only man in the place. The others are caffeinated mothers who have just dropped their children off at school. There are whoops of laughter now and then. The next table is talking about where to get the best burrata.

So thank you, Todd, but I can't do coffee for a bit. As I said, I am writing a book.

Love,
Jeffrey

# ARE YOU ANYBODY?

## Red Bowtie

I grew up in San Francisco, a magical place. Our first house was on Thirty-First Street, which meant we were thirty-one blocks and change from the Pacific Ocean. It was foggy every morning, clear or overcast and sixty degrees every afternoon, and the fog rolled back in on the dot at 5:00 p.m. The fog was moody and lovely and taught me to love inclement weather. That's why Los Angeles and I never got along; it's sunny all the time. I am the Jewish son of Russian Hungarian parents. I can't have sunny all the time.

My maternal grandparents, Yossel and Gertrude Salzberg, lived nearby, and my grandmother would sometimes babysit for me when my parents were away. She would bring her homemade pickles— dill, half-sour, garlic. She brought matzoh and gefilte fish and herring. One time, she brought this wonderful cocoa. She put a pot of milk on the stove, spooned in the cocoa and a little sugar, and stirred and stirred and stirred. When it was ready, she handed me a mug of it. Bliss.

That same weekend, she brought me a gift—a red bowtie. To this day, I have absolutely no idea why. It was big and shiny and I loved it.

My parents used to take me out to dinner with them. We'd all get dressed up, me in my charcoal suit, white shirt, and that big beautiful red bowtie. We would eat at Joe's of Westlake and order the legendary Joe's special: scrambled eggs, ground meat, and spinach. But before we ate, my parents liked to have a drink at the bar in the lounge. I wasn't allowed to sit at the bar, so I would sit at a table by myself near the piano player, sipping my Shirley Temple. I loved to watch people, study their mannerisms and their gestures. It was as good as reading a book. A dark book with piano music and cigarette smoke. My parents couldn't get over the fact that I never complained that we didn't eat until 9:00 p.m.

People would come up to me and say, "Hello, little boy. What a beautiful bowtie." And get this: they would give me money. Not pennies, not quarters, not half-dollars—they gave me dollar bills. Some sat down to talk to me and tell me their stories. I became used to the smell of alcohol on their breath. One doctor sat down with me and told me about a patient he had lost that day; he had a martini with two olives in his hand and tears in his eyes.

I couldn't get over all the attention, the stories, the sharing. I knew it wasn't because of me. It was because of **it**—the bowtie had magical power; this red glittery thing made me feel confident and wise. I felt connected. I felt powerful. I felt helpful. I felt safe.

I took that feeling with me when I walked to school or around my neighborhood. I felt it when my mom got me a new pair of Keds, and I would run around the neighborhood feeling like I was the fastest creature on earth. I remember thinking, **This is the fastest I will ever be—ever.** I even woke my parents up early one morning to tell them just that. They were unimpressed.

I used to go to the Soap Box Derby races with my brother and my father every weekend. They were held outside the Harding Park golf course, not far from our house. My brother and dad and I would watch the kids get in their go-karts at the top of the hill, and I was able to tell which one would win just by how the driver sat in the car. During each and every race, I would guess the winner, and I got it right every time. People started to place bets based on my guesses. "Which one, son?" People were making money on my say-so, including my dad and brother. I was invincible.

And then one night when I was about eight years old, I was getting dressed in my little suit to go to Joe's of Westlake and I couldn't find my red bowtie. I searched and searched, but no red bowtie. I went to my mother to see if she knew where it was.

"Come on, Jeffrey! We're late."

"I can't find my red bowtie."

"What red bowtie?"

"My red bowtie. The one Grandma gave me."

"Grandma never gave you—"

"I wear a red bowtie! I always wear a red bowtie!"

"There is no red bowtie. You've never had a red bowtie."

I was speechless.

"You have a small blue bowtie," she said. "That's the only one you have. Go put it on, and hurry!"

I went to my room and got the little blue bowtie and we went to Joe's. I sat with my Shirley Temple near the piano player as usual, but nobody talked to me. No one approached. Nobody gave me money. Nobody sat down and told me their story. Even the piano player was silent.

I began to feel an unfamiliar sensation in the middle of my chest—fear. My connection to the world was gone. My red bowtie was gone. Not only gone, it may have never existed. Now when we went to the Soap Box Derby, I was clueless about who would win. And when I walked around the neighborhood, I was afraid.

I would spend the rest of my life looking for that red bowtie, trying to connect to that feeling it gave me, that access, that magic. I sometimes struggle to find it, and on occasion I do, and in the most unexpected places—onstage, on a set, in a grocery store, behind the wheel of a car in a strange town, in a book, as a sidekick, as twin brothers, and, to no one's surprise more than mine, as a woman.

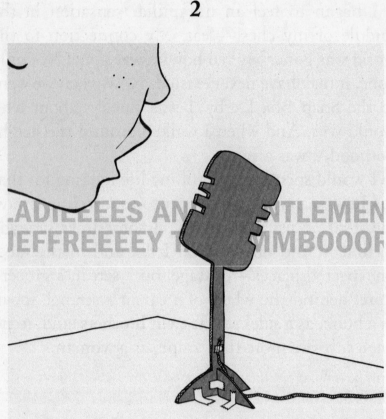

## 2

# Are You Anybody?

L ike lots of American families in the '50s, we would gather around the black-and-white television and watch **Tonight Starring Jack Paar.** I thought Mr. Paar was incredible and his regular guests, like Dody Goodman, Pat Weaver,

Charley Weaver (a.k.a. Clifford Arquette—David, Patricia, and Rosanna Arquette's grandfather), were hilarious, but the driest, wittiest of them all was the gentleman who played piano, Oscar Levant. He was the master of one-liners. Jack Paar would ask him, "What do you do for exercise?" and Mr. Levant would answer: "I stumble and then I fall into a coma." I was in awe of how he did so much with so little and sent Jack Paar into convulsions of laughter. It was a skill I would remember and forget throughout my career, doing so little to get so much.

There was Jack Benny, whom I loved. He would do nothing, just put his hand under his chin and turn toward the camera with this expression on his face. The people around him—Don Wilson, Mel Blanc—would be outrageous, but Mr. Benny would just turn to us and blink, and we would collapse helplessly.

All of these people on the television were so happy and witty and elegant and sophisticated. I was enthralled by this vision of a happier life right in front of me in black and white. To me, it seemed as though they all came to the show from some wonderful ongoing "ball," and right after the show, when the Tambors went to bed, they would go right back to the party.

I loved Steve Allen's afternoon show too, which I turned on every day after school at 4:00 p.m. while all my peers were watching **American Bandstand** with Dick Clark. First, Steve Allen looked just like my drama teacher at Aptos Junior High School, Mr. "Prav." Second, he did this thing where he yelled, "Smock! Smock!" in a high falsetto for no reason whatsoever, and I thought it was the funniest thing ever. He was immensely clever and debonair, as though he too had taken time out from the ball to spend time with this husky, lisping Jewish kid in San Francisco. His sidekick, Louis Nye, would say, "Hi-ho, Steve-a-rino!" and I laughed every time. I began to worship "silly." Only the bravest and best and the brightest dared go there. **See also:** Ernie Kovacs, Mel Brooks, Carl Reiner, Lou Costello, Red Skelton (his Clem Kadiddlehopper was life-changing).

Then Steve Allen would stop all this silliness and step over to the piano and just play, usually something sort of plain and simple and serious. There were no rules to this show. It went where they went, and it was tremendously fun. "Enthralled" doesn't begin to explain how I felt when watching this man perform.

I longed to be famous enough to be invited on those splendid talk shows. I wanted to go to the ball. I practiced signing my autograph: "Best wishes, Jeffrey Tambor." "All my very best to you, Jeffrey Tambor." "Thanks, Jeffrey Tambor." "Wishing you the best, Jeffrey Tambor." "Hi there, Jeffrey Tambor." One day my third-grade teacher, Mrs. Fischer, at Westlake Elementary School found a piece of paper I'd been practicing on. "Jeffrey, are you signing **autographs**?"

After school, I used to go down to the basement, where I arranged a desk and two chairs, one behind the desk and one beside it, and I would do my own talk show. I had made a microphone out of cardboard. First I would be the host and address the "camera," then I'd welcome my guest and run over to the guest chair. Then I'd go back to the host chair behind the desk and ask my guest a question, then run back to the guest chair to answer. I would also imitate the sound of the audience laughing, which sounded a lot like a phlegmy cat hissing in its last stages. My parents would hear this from upstairs. I'm surprised they didn't try to arrange an exorcism.

One night I was watching Jack Paar with my parents and my brother in the den, which was on the third floor of our house. I was sitting at my father's knee, and we were all laughing. When the show cut to commercial, I announced to the room, "I'm going to be on the **Tonight** show one day."

Nobody laughed or made fun of me. My father just said, "Ah, Bep."

My nickname was Bep, which was short for Beppy, because I couldn't say Jeffrey when I was a child, so I called myself Beppy. My father called me Bep until the day he died. Sometimes he called me Stinky, too, especially in front of my girlfriends. "Be careful tonight, Stinky," he'd say to my mortification as I headed out for a date.

I revered my father. He was a big man, six foot three, and a lefty like me. He'd been an amateur boxer on the Lower East Side of Manhattan, where he grew up under the elevated train. He earned extra money going a few rounds with up-and-coming professional boxers, including, legend had it, Joe Louis. In my father's telling of the story, he never saw Louis's left hook coming, he just remembered waking up on the mat. After that, Dad could only breathe out of one nostril and had sinus problems plus a clicking jaw for the rest of his life.

When my father moved to San Francisco, he turned professional light heavyweight. Another legend has it that he boxed one of the Baer brothers, Max or Buddy. I don't know if it was really true or just bullshit. But I used to watch the Pabst Blue Ribbon Wednesday-night fights with him. My father's hero was Archie Moore, who defended himself in a crouch the same way my father had.

When my father said, "Ah, Bep," in response to my announcement that I would one day be on television, he reached out to give me a playful smack on the top of my head, but his ring hit me and it really, really hurt. I don't know if it was my father's failure to recognize my genuine desire, that he failed to see **me,** or if it was the bolt of pain from his ring, but I burst into tears.

And **then** the laughter started. My father, my mother, and my brother were all laughing.

The great cellist Yo-Yo Ma once said that you have

to have fire in the belly to be an artist. Same goes for being an actor. It's not enough to **want** to be an actor, you have to have that fire. One of the things that provided that fire for me was that moment with my family. I loved my dad, but I was going to prove him wrong. I woke each morning with a mission, with fire in the belly.

Many years later, in the mid-1990s, my father having long since died, I was standing in the wings at NBC Studios in Burbank, about to make my first appearance on **The Tonight Show with Jay Leno.** I looked up and pointed skyward with my index finger and said, "That's one."

To be fair, my dad did take me and Larry to see all the sights in Hollywood once. We visited Television City, where my hero Red Skelton did his show. And we strolled the Walk of Fame and put our hands in the prints of all the stars at Grauman's Chinese Theatre. I've just been told I am to receive my own star this year on the Hollywood Walk of Fame, so I guess "that's two" for Dad.

One of my other goals was to be on the cover of **Time** magazine by the age of thirty-five. Which was tough, because when it didn't happen, I thought, **Oh well, thirty-six then.** Then thirty-seven. By forty, I thought, **You know what? I'm going to sub-scribe to another magazine, because this ain't happening.**

The truth is, male or female, we all grow up with this preconception that we are Cinderella, and all we want is to be invited to the ball. For me, I thought, if I could only sign an autograph, my life would finally have meaning. Long before I shook Jay Leno's hand for the first time, I had a small part on Broadway in a comedy called **Sly Fox.** It was my first Broadway show, at the Broadhurst Theatre on Forty-Fourth Street. The show playing to our right was **My Fair Lady** and the show to our left was **A Chorus Line.** Let's just say it was a busy street.

I had just three lines in the play, but I felt like I'd arrived. I bought myself a gorgeous $300 ankle-length faux cashmere coat from Bloomingdale's. I wore a hat at a rakish angle. Let me reiterate: I had three lines. In fact, it was the same line said three times.

Fans would congregate by the stage door hoping to catch the actors on their way out and get an autograph. There was one guy who went from theater to theater every night with pad in hand, stopping actors on their way out, "Are you anybody?"

Long pause. "No."

He kept walking.

It would be three more years before I finally got to write my name on a piece of paper for a fan. It was March 14, 1979, and I was coming out of the Forty-Fourth Street exit of the Times Square subway station and I heard, "Hey, there's that guy on TV!" because **The Ropers** had premiered on ABC at 9:00 p.m. the night before. I died—I was a

TV actor, the anathema of my college and repertory days. I stood on that top stair and he asked for my autograph and handed me a scrap of paper. "Best wishes, Jeffrey Tambor." He didn't even look at it, just folded it and stuck it in his pocket. It wasn't how I imagined it at all. In the distance, I thought I could just make out Peggy Lee singing, "Is that all there is?"

In the years since, I've been approached while eating dinner, picking my kids up from school, getting coffee at Dunkin' Donuts, filling up at gas stations, but I never say no.

My friend and mentor Henry Winkler is the nicest person in the world. Let me repeat, Henry Winkler is the **nicest** person in the world. He's nice to everybody. He says, "Thank you, that was delicious" to the flight attendant who clears his tray. He signs autographs, he agrees to take selfies with fans. He'll go, "Heyyyyy," as the Fonz, if he's asked. I asked him how he was always so generous with fans, and he said, "Remember, Jeffrey. It's your five hundredth time, but it's their first."

Not long ago, I was teaching an advanced acting class in Los Angeles—this was serious craft, not for **pishers**—and I said, just out of curiosity, "How many of you want to be famous?" Everybody raised their hands.

Recently my wife, Kasia, and I were returning home from what they call an A-list party, a very nice affair, not a pigs-in-blankets kind of deal. Kasia asked me what was wrong—she can read me so well.

"I wish I knew," I said.

"Knew what?"

"It's just a party," I said.

"Yes, what did you expect?" she said.

"I don't know. I thought it would be . . . more."

**3**

# Bar Mitzvahed at Gunpoint

There are three kinds of Jews: Orthodox Jews, who only read Hebrew; Conservative Jews, who read Hebrew and English; and Reform Jews, whose only requirement is to sing show tunes. "Tomorrow" from **Annie** is especially well regarded.

The Tambors were Conservative Jews, the only Jewish family for miles. To me, being Jewish just meant "otherness." One day after school, I was visiting a girl I was friends with from Westlake Elementary School, and her mother yelled downstairs, "Jane, who's here with you?"

"Jeffrey Tambor," Jane said.

"Come upstairs."

When Jane came back downstairs, she said, "Mother says you have to go."

"Why?"

"Because my mom says you are the people who killed Christ."

I gathered my books and walked back down the hill to my house.

At dinner that night, I told my parents what had happened. My parents, who were as desperate to assimilate as all their Jewish friends, didn't say a word. But I could tell by their look—they were terrified.

The Tambors attended Temple Beth Shalom at Fourteenth Avenue and Clement Street. The synagogue smelled like wool after it's rained. On the High Holy Days, especially Yom Kippur, you're not supposed to brush your teeth, so we had the double whammy of the wet sheep smell and halitosis. So you can't understand Hebrew and you're trying to control your gag reflex. Other than that, it was fine.

My parents only went to temple when they had to, but Larry and I had to go to Hebrew school on Sundays. We always stopped at Foster's Cafeteria for pancakes and bacon on the way. Larry was the uber-Jew. He was president of the congregation, and he studied his heart out. I struggled with it. None of my friends at Westlake Elementary went to Hebrew school. Not one.

Why do **I** have to be singled out by my friends? Why do **I** have to be the killer of Christ? Why does Grandpa Yossel have to have a nose like that? Why do **I** have to be in the car when someone yells "Kike!" at my mother and she pulls over and starts weeping?

What really got me was the title of the book we were assigned to read by Mr. Weiner, our teacher. It was called **When the Jewish People Was Young.** I couldn't get past how wrong that sounded.

In class, Mr. Weiner asked, "Any questions?"

I raised my hand immediately.

"Big questions take time, Jeffrey."

This couldn't wait. "Why is the book called this?"

"What do you mean?"

"Why is it called **When the Jewish People Was Young**?"

"What's the problem?"

"Shouldn't it be **When the Jewish People** Were **Young**?"

"No, it's **When the Jewish People** Was **Young**."

It sounded so immigrant to me, like someone

who'd just gotten off the boat, which was my problem with Judaism—I didn't want to be different.

"I have one more question," I said to Mr. Weiner.

"Okay, what is it?"

"No, forget it."

"Big questions are important, Jeffrey. Is it a big question?"

"It **is** a big question."

"All right. Take your time."

"Mr. Weiner?"

"Yes, Jeffrey?"

"How do we know there's a God?"

"Get out!" Mr. Weiner yelled, and gestured toward the door. He threw me out of Hebrew school.

I didn't want my parents to know I'd been kicked out that day, so after that I still went to shul with Larry every Sunday, clutching my copy of **When the Jewish People Was Young,** but I refused to go inside. Instead, I'd walk around the Richmond District just off Golden Gate Park. There was nothing fancy about the neighborhood, but it had bakeries. Lots and lots of bakeries—Ukrainian, Lithuanian, Hungarian—and the thing they all had in common was cream. Every week I'd get a cream-filled pastry and gain weight waiting for my dad to pick us up. I **ate** Fourteenth and Clement.

One Sunday, I heard singing coming from upstairs at the synagogue. I went in and found a seat on a back bench and watched. I was alone except for the old man my brother and I called the **haysedon-dere.** We called him that because whenever we got to running around the synagogue, he would yell at us, "Hey! Hey! Sit down dere!"

Up at the altar, there were men with yarmulkes and shawls sitting in a row of chairs. One after the other, they would rise and sing. Apparently a cantor from another synagogue had died and they were holding an audition for a replacement. So I was there with my cream-crammed pastry in one hand and **When the Jewish People Was Young** in the other, and I dissolved into tears at the beauty of the singing. It reminded me of Grandpa's Jan Peerce recordings of "Eli Eli" and "Kaddish." Peerce was an opera singer but he also sang cantorial songs. To this day, you put on a Jan Peerce record and I'm done. I was transfixed by the way these men broke their voices and used both guttural and lyrical effects in the songs. The sheer beauty of their singing made me feel safe.

I left the synagogue thinking, **I've got it. I'll be a cantor.**

I went home and told my parents everything: how much I didn't like the whole Jewish deal, that Jewish people look different from everyone else. I confessed to being dismissed from class and how I watched the auditions and now I wanted to be a cantor.

Then I asked my father, "What is it cantors sing?"

He explained that they were telling stories about how to survive, and that these stories had saved Jews' lives. "You'll have to learn Hebrew."

Okay, so I wouldn't be a cantor. But this telling of stories . . . these stories.

My grandparents lived at 54 Grove Street in downtown San Francisco, and they hosted the family Seder every Passover. When I was a kid, we used to have matzoh with butter, which I believe is illegal. I love it. It's low in calories, even if it does taste pretty much like you're eating one of those graduation mortarboard hats. On the other hand, it has a good crunch to it. I'm all about crunch. (I'm a joke in my house because I put pretzels in my soup and rice cakes crumbled up in my salad.) Anyway, in those days, there were only two kinds of matzoh on my grandmother's Seder table—regular, down by my grandpa's seat; and egg, by us. I thought the egg matzoh was kind of strange, like having Dunkin' Donuts on the table.

Passover today isn't like it was sixty years ago. Now, there's spelt matzoh. There's gluten-free matzoh. There is lite matzoh, which I'm surprised doesn't have a Weight Watchers points-number listed on the package. The kicker is the bran matzoh—it's matzoh that will not only send you to heaven but will make you lighter for the trip.

Grandma was named Gertrude Salzberg and Grandpa was Yossel Joseph, and they were both from Ukraine. Legend has it that my grandpa hid out from the Cossacks, then got on a train, then got on a ship to come to the United States. I've heard that same story so many times from Ukrainian refugees that I think everyone's borrowing from one Ur-story.

My grandfather was a bookbinder, which may be where my love for books comes from. (There weren't any books in my house growing up; my dad read **Reader's Digest** and my mom kept a copy of a sex manual in her bedside table.) Grandpa got up at four o'clock every morning and had a glass of hot water and a hard-boiled egg for breakfast. He came home at three o'clock in the afternoon, and my grandmother had a piece of rye bread and a schnapps waiting for him. He was a handsome man with a full head of hair and an almost Italianate hooked nose. He looked more Renaissance than Shylockean. He tried to be gruff, but he wasn't very good at it because he had such a gentle soul.

So my grandparents hosted the Seder every year, and the whole family would come: Barney, Eileen, Larry, and Jeffrey Tambor; Aunt Mitzi and Uncle Bill with cousins Harvey, Adrianne, and Stevie Salzberg; Aunt Lee and Uncle Hy with cousins Barbara and Roger Gold; and bringing up the rear was Uncle Leonard and his wife Althea (who everybody referred to as the "shiksa") and their kids, Michael and Robbie Salzberg. Althea was a peroxide-blond hairdresser, and Uncle Leonard had given up a "respectable profession" to become a hairdresser as well. As a Tambor, you were expected to roll your eyes at anything Althea said.

The Tambors and the Salzbergs didn't always have a warm and fuzzy relationship, but the kids all loved one another. One Seder, two of my aunts got into a fistfight—we hadn't even sat down. Yossel was apoplectic.

So we sat around the long table, not speaking to each other but trying to be on our best behavior as we read from the Haggadah, which is the tale of the Jews' exodus from Egypt. (It's a long tale of survival. It is not like **The Ten Things You Need to Know About Survival,** or **The Idiot's Guide to How the Jews Survived.** And it's in Hebrew.) As the reading went on and on, you felt hunger so bad you wanted to kill yourself for a good two hours while Grandpa droned on about God knew what.

I was nervous because 1) I barely understood it; and 2) as the youngest, I had to read the Four Questions, or as they're called in Yiddish **di fir kashes.** And that part didn't come until a good forty minutes in, with all the stops along the way. First there was the blessing over the wine—that awful Manischewitz, which isn't served for nearly half an hour. As a little kid, it's already past your bedtime and you're tired and groggy, so that little glass of sweet wine without having eaten leaves you schnockered. And you still have the Four Questions to recite.

When it was finally time, I had a little secret to ingratiate myself with Grandpa (after all, we still had Hide the Matzoh, upon which dollars hinged, coming up). I had learned in Hebrew school how to say the beginning to the Four Questions in Yiddish. I began: "Grandpa, I will ask you the Four Questions." **Tata, ich wil fregen di fir kashes.**

I was a hit. People ooohed and aaaahed. Althea tried to smile. There were grudging looks of admiration/hatred amongst my mother's sisters, and envy from the cousins.

Next was the egg, then the bitter herbs, then the ubiquitous matzoh with a little sweet paste made from nuts and apples on it called **choroset.** My grandpa took over reading the section called **Is That Not Sufficient?** It went like this:

The Jews went through such and such. **Is that not sufficient? Dayenu.**

Then the Jews went through this other thing. **Is that not sufficient? Dayenu.**

And it went on like that. I knew that when we got to the final **dayenu,** it was ten minutes until touchdown. The reading would be over and my grandmother would get up and go in the kitchen to heat up the food. **Dayenu** meant we would finally eat.

First on the menu was gefilte fish—hot the first night, cold the second (yep, we did this two nights in a row). It was delicious. My grandmother's recipe was made with fresh carp. How do I know? I saw the live carp Grandma put in the bathtub the week before. (Every week there'd be something in the bathtub. One week it was pickles, another it was the biggest enema bag I've ever seen in my life.) The gefilte fish was served with a slice of carrot on top and purple horseradish on the side and matzoh. Heaven arrived with the next course: chicken soup with a matzoh ball the size of Pittsburgh. Fresh chicken, beautifully cooked, so succulent. And then Grandma did something I've never encountered anywhere else. She put together cold fruit—prunes, peaches, apricots, apples, grapes—all sliced and ice cold—and made it into a compote. I've never had anything equal to it.

Then we played Hide the Matzoh. Not Find the Matzoh. And here's the thing: Grandpa **really** hid the matzoh. No one could ever find it, and he wouldn't tell us where it was. I don't know if he thought it was a breach of ethics or something, but he wouldn't say a peep and **we never found the matzoh.**

Then we would all kiss each other on the cheek and say good-bye—except for Althea, you don't kiss the shiksa—and we went home, Larry and I always falling asleep in the backseat of the car on the way.

**CUT TO:** Eighth grade. Every Wednesday after school, I would take the bus across town to study for my bar mitzvah with the humorless Cantor Bornstein, or as I liked to call him, Cantor Bore-stein. I had such a hard time learning the Torah that he made me a recording to memorize. I could have lip-synched my bar mitzvah. Mrs. Bore-stein made him cottage cheese sandwiches on toast, which she left for him in a paper bag. He'd take a bite, and then we'd recite the Torah together.

If you've ever heard Hebrew, you know that whenever someone says a word like **baruch,** that "ch" sound is guttural. It's not "ba-ruck." It's "ba-**roochhh.**" You have to really hit that last bit. I would say "ba-ruck," and Cantor Bore-stein would correct me midbite: "It's ba-**rooch**! Ba-**rooch**!" and curds of cottage cheese would go hurtling through the air and onto me. By the end of the lesson, I would look like one of those popcorn ceilings in the newer homes in the Valley. To this day, I feel a strong connection between Judaism and milk products.

Rabbi Saul White called my dad about my progress. "Barney, I gotta tell you, it's not going well."

"He'll be fine," my father would say.

Six months of teaching, and it was Saturday morning—the day of my bar mitzvah. I was dreading it. I was extremely nervous. To make matters worse, I had an aversion to wool. Our tailor didn't do that fancy thing of lining a suit and I couldn't stand the feel of the wool next to my skin. So, unbeknownst to my mom or dad, I was wearing flannel pajama bottoms under my charcoal gray suit. It looked like there was something terribly wrong with me from the waist down.

When we got to the synagogue, my mother pointed to my name on the sign outside: BAR MITZVAH BOY JEFFREY TAMBOR WILL DO THE HAFTORAH. "There you are, up in lights."

"Are you nervous?" she asked.

"Well, yes, of course I'm nervous."

And she said these fateful words: "Here, let me give you something."

Miltown was the Xanax of its day. It was much prescribed and much used. Humorist S. J. Perelman even wrote a book called **The Road to Miltown.** My mother handed me the round pill and I took it. Long story short, I was high at my bar mitzvah.

I went up to the podium and my father came up and put his arms around me. The rabbi opened the Torah. Most bar mitzvah boys do a five- or ten-minute story out of the Talmud in Hebrew, but the selection that was indicated for me—which is based on your birth date—was the size of Edward Gibbon's **The History of the Decline and Fall of the Roman Empire.** (Any Jews born on July 8 about to be bar mitzvahed, run as fast as you can, or change to Reform and you can sing **Annie** instead.)

But wait, that's not all! This Torah didn't look anything like what I'd been studying. In Cantor Bore-stein's office, the Torah we used had diacritical marks on the text, so you'd know how to pronounce the words. So now I was both confused and woozy. I said the first line, and the entire congregation of damp wool said, "Amen" like the chorus of the Metropolitan Opera. It was thunderous compared to the simple "Amen" Borestein would mutter with the cottage cheese in the corners of his mouth.

I had memorized the haftorah, but, with the full congregation's "Amen," it fell out of my brain, onto the floor, and went back to the car. In the theater, we would call that "You're up." You're up on your lines. This was my first "up." But there was no stage manager to help throw you your lines. I was on my own. It was me and God and **When the Jewish People Was Young.**

I started to improvise. What came out of me was some kind of cacophonous mixture of Jan Peerce, Jerry Lewis, and Ella Fitzgerald scat singing. I was making up sounds. Cantor Bore-stein's eyes were getting wider and wider. Finally, I made my way back to earth and Temple Beth Shalom, and I settled into it.

By the time I got to my speech, I was full-on wrecked from the Miltown, so I went off-book there, too. I decided to speak from my heart. It was a real performance. I talked about being a young Jew. Lies upon lies upon lies. I said I wanted to be a cantor when I grew up. I said hello to my friend Terry Black in the back row—"You look great!" People were crying at the sincerity of my beautiful speech.

And that has been my relationship with Judaism ever since: a book that was named incorrectly, cottage cheese, Miltown, and the most beautiful stories being sung by auditioning cantors upstairs in a tiny shul, breaking my heart and giving me faith.

CUT TO: In the wake of shooting the worst film

of my career in Nice, France, my wife, Kasia, and
I were taking a monthlong break in Kraków, Poland, where Kasia was going to school to polish her
Polish. When we checked in to our hotel, the con-
cierge gave us a brochure highlighting all the local
"doings" and "must-sees" in this beautiful university town. On the list with cathedrals and museums
was nearby Auschwitz-Birkenau.

"I'm not sure I want to go," I said to Kasia the
night before we were to go.

"You have to go."

"I don't know if I can."

"You have to go."

The universe started sending signs immediately.
About halfway there, our driver's brand-new Mer-
cedes broke down. He got out of the car and popped
the hood. A minute later, he was crying. The car
was dead. He called his friend to take us the rest of
the way.

We waited by the side of the road. Every few minutes, I'd look at Kasia.

"You have to go."

An hour later, our substitute ride came and we
continued our journey.

Then we were there. Kasia stepped out of the car
and had an immediate attack of migraine, the pain
remaining through the day. I stepped out of the car
and felt nothing, dead.

The entry is still the same. The words **arbeit
macht frei**—WORK SETS YOU FREE—adorn the arch

over the gate. Hannah Arendt had it bang on the head when she wrote about the banality of evil in describing Adolf Eichmann's trial and execution in Israel. I had played the head of the Mossad in **The Man Who Captured Eichmann,** opposite Robert Duvall. The film was shot in Argentina, partly on the street where Eichmann was hiding out before his capture. This experience was utterly different. This was not a set.

The images of men and women were lined up along the walls, stretching the length of the corridor, all expressionless, eyes dead, dressed in striped jackets, the men in hats. No screaming, no horror, just desolation. The faces not sad, not scared, just gone, disappeared. There were no children. **They didn't take pictures of children?**

Another room off the corridor featured a wooden table, four wooden chairs, a window. Farther down the corridor, a big plate-glass window. Behind it, stacks of luggage, bags representing all economic echelons piled one atop the other almost to the ceiling. Down the next corridor, the next plate-glass window: shoes. **Oh my God.** Shoes of all sizes. Little ones. A pile almost to the top of the room.

Everywhere we went, there was a chair, a photograph, a book, a shoe, a coat, a hat with a feather, a bandanna. I saw an Italian family taking a photograph in front of one of the barracks. They posed with their arms around each other, smiling. **Click.** Smile. **Click.**

There was a cafeteria offering food and drink for tourists, sandwiches and desserts.

Steven Bochco told me a story when I was working on **Hill Street Blues.** Walter Matthau and his wife, Carol, had planned a visit to Auschwitz during a trip to Kraków. According to the story, Walter and Carol got into a heated argument the night before in their hotel room. The next day, they got into their car and drove silently the hour and a half to Auschwitz. When they got to the camps, they took separate tours, Carol to one camp, Walter to another, then switched. Carol was so stricken, she begged Walter to forgive her during the drive back to their hotel.

"Oh great, Carol, after ruining Auschwitz for me."

Kasia and I got back into the car. We didn't talk much. Kasia was quite sick with her migraine. I was totally out of my body. "It was the shoes," she said, that's where she broke. I didn't break. I still felt nothing.

Two weeks later, back in Los Angeles in our home by the ocean, I made my weekly trip to Dr. Ron up in Topanga Canyon.

"How was Auschwitz?" he asked.

A tear started to rip in my chest and I began to groan, louder and louder, and then sob. I collapsed in Dr. Ron's arms.

"Larry. Larry. Larry," I kept saying.

There are rites of passages. For me, my bar mitzvah was not one of them, although it is the ritual entrance to the community. That day in Poland, that was my initiation.

I keep a photograph folded in my wallet of a little Jewish boy being marched out of the Warsaw ghetto at gunpoint. When I lose my nerve, I take the photo out and look at it. I am that boy. We are all that boy.

A reporter once asked me if I put my Jewish roots in my performances.

"All my characters are Jewish," I said.

# 4

## My Story

After I graduated from San Francisco State College, I went to Wayne State University in Detroit for my graduate degree, which, let's be honest, made no sense. I wanted to be an actor. You don't need a graduate degree for that, and in downtown Detroit, no less.

Jim Thompson was my advisor at SFSC. He was from Minnesota, and all his cronies from back home were faculty at Wayne State. Dr. Jim and a tape recording of my breathless four-minute interpretation of the "If it were done, when 'tis done, then 'twere **well** [I emphasized "well," which they considered revolutionary], it were done quickly" speech from **Macbeth** got me a scholarship, $55 a week, and all the inner-city poverty I could handle.

As part of my scholarship, I performed in the repertory company, took classes toward a master's degree, and taught an acting class. I was twenty years old, and I've been teaching ever since. I taught at Wayne State for five years, then taught for the esteemed director and coach Milton Katselas for two decades at his famed Beverly Hills Playhouse, then held an acting workshop at SXSW for ten years.

For the last few years, I've been on the road with a program I call "Performing Your Life," which is the fancy-schmantzy name I made up for it while eating pastrami at Art's Delicatessen in Studio City, in answer to Michael Laskin's question "What shall we call this?" (Michael was my producer at the time.) Lately, I added a little coda to the schmantzy name of my talk: "Performing Your Life: What's Keeping You?" This coda is a fascination of mine. I am consumed by why people stop. Just stop. And move to "more comfortable rooms." Change directions and give up.

Here's the deal. I have taught thousands of students over the years—some successful students, and some very, very successful students. I've had some students who have become very wealthy—one billionaire and many millionaires—and the rest, I guess, are thousandaires. Some have won major awards. But 90 percent of my students abandoned their acting dreams to settle for "other rooms of less consequence." I've become obsessed with why so many of us halt our progress, fold up the cards, call it a day.

At the start of my lecture, no matter where I am, whether it's a university or some corporate function, I dedicate my talk to a late friend of mine who came up to me one day with tears in his eyes and said, "I used to be somebody. Now I've become somebody else. God help me, what have I done?"

I used to pitch for my Cub Scout softball team,

the Westlake Tigers, Pack 248. Our uniforms were bought by Woody's Barber Shop in the shopping center across the highway. The uniforms were magnificent, white and pristine—pristine because none of the team ever slid or had any contact with anything brown or green like you're supposed to when you're playing baseball. The catcher was Peter Dunan. Mr. Dunan, his father, was the coach. When I was pitching and things were going awry—there was not a strike to be seen or called by the umpire—Mr. Dunan would call time out, and he and Peter would come out to the pitcher's mound and Mr. Dunan would say, "What's keeping you, son?"

Old-fashioned merry-go-rounds sometimes had a dispenser or wooden arm with brass rings, and riders tried to snatch a ring as they passed it. It's become a symbol for taking what you want, even if you have to lean precariously off your horse to get it. I want to know what keeps us from that ring. I think the answer is a story, a story that keeps us from the prize. (I'm not the first person to think this, for those of you playing along at home.)

In my talk, I speak about an actress who was in one of my acting workshops. She was terrific, one of the best students I ever had, dazzling, except anytime we worked on a scene from a Tennessee Williams play or other material that had any sexual connotation, she couldn't "bring" it. She would get right up to the mark—and freeze. I could see her practically leave her body and go soft and squeamish.

After a scene, I would invite the actors to sit at the edge of the stage to talk about their performance—what they were working on . . . how they think they did . . . what their process was . . . that stuff. During one of these talks/critiques/back-and-forths, I asked her the Mr. Dunan special: "What's holding you back?" She talked about the usual things: where she grew up back East, where she lived now in Los Angeles, how she came out here to try acting, that kind of thing. And she happened to mention in passing that she spoke to her father on the phone almost every night, and at the end of every call before he hung up, he said, "Are you still my little girl?"

Houston, I believe we have a story. How could she ever be comfortable with her attack on a scene with that daddy whispering in her ear with every move she made? That story gets up with her in the morning, chooses her outfit for the day, and goes to rehearsal with her. It hangs around until it's time to accompany her home and wait for the phone call.

Here's another. I had a student who was the brother of a very successful businessman. And he would jest he was the unsuccessful brother. That's his role, the role he has adopted for his life. He has an unsuccessful car, he has unsuccessful clothes, he has an unsuccessful agent, he has an unsuccessful house. And he has an unsuccessful career. The story affects your life.

When I do my talk, I choose a moment in the

evening to have the audience close their eyes and imagine someone in their lives who is having a bad time of it, someone who is failing. I caution them not to use themselves, because it's too close and it's hard to be objective. It's quite a sight to see this from the stage, and it is so affecting to see people getting in touch with their feelings about their friends and their pain. It is very quiet, because we all realize in that instant that there are manufactured and inherited stories that keep us from the prize.

Want another?

My dad, Bernard no-middle-name Tambor—they didn't give him a middle name—Barney on the West Coast, Bernie on the East—came from a Hungarian Jewish family (our part of Hungary was in Prussia at the time) who lost people in the Holocaust. How he passed that on to me was: "Shhh, shhh, shhh. Don't celebrate. They'll take it away from you." He would always tell me, "Keep your nose clean." Stay out of trouble. Stay below the radar. Don't celebrate. Shhh.

It's worth noting that the very definition of being an actor is: Don't keep your nose clean—your mission is to get **into** trouble and stay there.

After Thirty-First Avenue, we moved to a community called Westlake in Daly City, just south of San Francisco. It was one of the first developments in the country designed specifically for working people, the brainchild of a genius developer named Henry Doelger. My father was a flooring contractor, and he had worked with Mr. Doelger when he was building this revolutionary community. We lived in one of these beautiful houses, which cost my parents $18,000, what I thought was a fortune. And we had a DeSoto two-door just like the one that was advertised on the Groucho Marx show, **You Bet Your Life.** Clearly, we were doing okay. When we said we were middle class, my mother would say, "No, no, we're upper-middle class."

The sun rose and set on my parents. My dad, the former boxer from the Lower East Side of New York, was big and handsome, like Cesar Romero. My mom, who came from Saint Paul, was Lena Horne beautiful and a fantastic cook. Every night when my dad got home from work, he'd take a shower and they'd dress up, turn on the radio, dance, and they would drink old-fashioneds with English bitters and smoke Lucky Strikes.

I adored my older brother, Larry. Lawrence Richard Tambor—him they gave a middle name. Five years older than me, he was the eldest and first boy child in a Jewish family. On his W2 form, it said "golden child." Everybody loved him. He wasn't just the troop leader of Pack 248 of the Boy Scouts, he was Order of the Arrow. Me, I got maybe the cooking merit badge. I think all I had to do was light a fire (I cheated, used a Zippo) and make beef stew out of a can. I ended up in the hospital after one camping trip because I was dehydrated and fell off a mule. So if there'd been a dehydration merit badge, I would have gotten that too. The mule was fine.

My mom was in charge of punishing us for our misdeeds. My dad never did it. The ex–professional boxer had no stomach for it. All he had to do was hold up his big boxer's hands and say, "These are lethal weapons," and Larry and I would scatter. But one time, my mother insisted he punish me after I'd broken a window in the kitchen, playing ball in the house.

"I don't want to hear any lecture about 'lethal weapons,'" she said. "You have to teach your son a lesson, Barney. Now."

My father solemnly ushered me upstairs to my bedroom and closed the door.

"Yell 'ow!'" he whispered, and slapped himself on the chest and arms.

**Slap!**

"Ow!"

**Slap!**

"Ow!"

"Cry, Bep," he whispered.

**Slap!**

"Ow!" and then in a whisper, "What?"

"Cry."

**Slap!**

"Ow!" I yelled, my voice breaking.

He nodded approval.

It was my first performance. We had created a "spanking" that never happened. I was delighted.

Okay, confession: I may have led you to believe those last few paragraphs are my story, but they're not. Those things happened, it's all true, but that's not my story. Close, but not quite.

Something happened in the Tambor family; something broke and stayed broken. It's the Tambor mystery. I have only fragments, hints, fuzzy memories.

**I'm in the car with my mother, driving across San Francisco. We arrive at a house I don't recognize. My mom and I get out of the car. We go upstairs to a waiting room. My aunt is there. My mom checks in with this woman. My aunt takes me to her house for the weekend.**

**My mom and her friend Eve Singer, a tough-talking Jewish girl, used to play golf together then go drink at Joe's of Westlake. One afternoon I got home from school, Eve was leaving. My mother was in the living room with a man. He looked familiar. Maybe the bartender at Joe's?**

**My dad packs up and leaves while Larry and I scream, "Don't go! Don't go!" He comes back a few weeks later. But now there is only silence and a sickening tension.**

My mom started acting different from the mom we had on the Avenues. She seemed to start drinking earlier and earlier in the day. She stopped making breakfast for us, instead locking herself in the bathroom with a vodka and lime juice.

"Bye, Mom."

Silence.

"Mom? Bye. I'm going to school [or **sshkool** with my lisp]."

Silence.

She still made dinner, enormous plates of food. I mean, **enormous**—I never knew what a normal serving looked like until I went to a restaurant. There was so much soup in a bowl, it was round, not flat. But my mother wouldn't eat. Instead, she would sit at the table with a drink and a Newport cigarette in silence. (Newports—who smokes Newports?) Not a word. She would just look at us as though she would have preferred we weren't there.

My poor dad's jaw clicked when he ate—either because of Joe Louis's left hook or undiagnosed TMJ—and my mother would turn to him as he clicked through the meal: "Barney." Larry got so nervous, he would crack his knuckles. She would turn to him: "Larry." She only looked at me; I didn't even get a "Jeffrey."

She would wait until late at night to cook herself a steak and a potato. She'd take it upstairs to her room and eat just a little bit in front of her television. Like clockwork, she fell asleep during the eleven o'clock news. I would go into her room, take the tray, go downstairs, and finish the steak and potato.

There came a time when my father sold our lovely house in Westlake because he needed the money to buy into a partnership at Floorcraft, the store where he worked, with his partners, Wally and Jack Lerner. We moved to an apartment in Parkmerced at 14 Vidal Street. It was a comedown for my mother, and things got worse. Much, much worse.

She started to break her silence. When she lost her temper, she would use words I never heard anybody else use. She said "fuck" and "shit" a lot— she was very fond of "shitty" this and "shitty" that, especially when examining my room and the ring in the bathtub. This was not a person I knew; it bore no resemblance to the mom on Thirty-First Avenue.

The house reeked of Lysol. Dad and the rest of us started eating over the kitchen sink to avoid making a mess. She had my dad install wall-to-wall **white** carpeting all over the house—including the bathroom. On top of the carpet, plastic runners everywhere, from entrance to exit. Woe unto you if she saw footprints on the runner—she could tell by shoe size who was the perp. We had to take off our shoes on entering the house, and put on these slippers that a Chinese acrobat might wear. There was plastic on all the furniture, and it was not even taken off for guests. I stopped inviting people over; I couldn't take the look on their faces when I pointed to the slippers they'd have to wear to play at Jeffrey's house.

When I was eighteen or nineteen, I was at home convalescing from a minor back surgery, when a group of my theater friends came by unexpectedly to visit me. I invited them in, shoes on, and had them take a seat on the sofa. From upstairs, my mother went crazy. "Who is down there? What the fuck are they doing? Get them out!" She threw in a lot of "shitty" and "fuck" to spice up the faceless rant from her bedroom. I will never forget the look on my friends' faces as they sheepishly left our house with my mother still yelling from upstairs.

About once a week, as a special treat at dinner, my mother would sit there, puffing on her cigarettes, and say ever so matter-of-factly:

**You are shtick drek.**
**You've always been shtick drek.**
**You will always be shtick drek.**

Translation:

**You are a piece of shit.**
**You've always been a piece of shit.**
**You will always be a piece of shit.**

It was a curse.
And that, ladies and gentlemen, is how you get yourself a story.
She cut ties with her family completely and abruptly. No more Seders with my grandparents.

"That piece of shit." "She's a piece of shit." The circle of the condemned was widening.

She inexplicably began to wear dark glasses at night. One evening at dinner, she said, "I wish you were dead." It was out of the blue—there was no antecedent to it. She wasn't looking at any one of us, she was just staring straight ahead.

**What is happening? Who is this? How do I make this stop? Where is the mom who dances to the radio?**

I was never threatened with physical violence. That would have been better. I would have killed for a beating. What she did was so much worse. It hurt.

Larry had left for college by the time my little sister, Jodi, was born. She never knew our warm, loving mother; she knew only this Gorgon, this hideous female monster whose look could turn you to stone, who was obviously in so much pain. My sister never had a chance.

One afternoon, I was in my bedroom with my sister watching cartoons on my black-and-white television, and my mother stopped in the doorway. She looked at us and gave us a smile, but not a warm and fuzzy one. And then she blew us a kiss. I could sense Jodi tensing. There was something ominous about it. My mother said nothing. The next thing we knew, she was being rushed to the hospital after trying to kill herself with an overdose of pills. She wasn't hospitalized, just given medication and sent home to drink even more, so she could try a second time.

We then entered what we fondly called the "your mother is very nervous" stage, which was my father's code phrase. Dad became terrified that she was going to commit suicide. We all were. Every action in the house was calibrated with: **Will this make her kill herself?** I still worry about this with students and friends to this day; this horrid measurement continues to be a part of my life, my story.

Dad would pick me up from school and tell me, "Your mother is very nervous." He'd be driving erratically, first at 5 mph and then 70 mph in a 25 mph zone, telling me over and over, "Your mother is very nervous, Stinky."

Then one day, my mother came into my bedroom as I was studying, and, without saying a word or any rancor in her expression, opened the window and proceeded to throw every single book I owned, including my schoolbooks and homework, out onto the street for all the world to see.

In that moment, I changed. I thought, **Whatever it takes, I will get out of here. I'm going to live.** I would steel myself, so that it wouldn't hurt anymore. I would never let anyone hurt me again; if I had to lie or manipulate or calculate, I would be cold of heart. As Iago said of his hatred of the Moor—I being Iago, my mother being the Moor—"I have't. It is engender'd. Hell and night must bring this monstrous birth to the world's light." I know,

I know, it's a little over the top, but when I first read this passage in college, I said to myself, "Yep, I get that. That's what I did!"

Actors have often said they have a problem with that aspect of Iago. Me? Piece of cake. It was my motto, the operating principle of my escape, Beppy's theme song. And that's why I am the last Tambor standing.

I'd looked up to Larry when I was a little boy, but that morphed a bit with the following incident. I had hauled in $400 from my bar mitzvah, which I kept in a passbook savings account at the Bank of America. I was so proud of that money, I would look at my bankbook every day. One day I went to the bank to withdraw ten dollars to buy myself something. The money was gone. All of it. I went to the bank manager, who was friends with my dad. He called Barney. Larry had pretended to be me, and took the money. All of it.

Larry, the golden child, was supposed to be the doctor in the family, but he didn't have the aptitude. He pretended he went to Princeton for college, but he didn't. He went away, but we didn't know where he went. In the end, the closest he got to fulfilling our parents' dream for him was by selling pharmaceutical supplies. He became alcoholic and obese. I went to a barbecue at his house in Martinez after I'd begun appearing on television. I sat there like I was the bee's knees. I knew he could sense the message I was sending him: **I beat you.** He had a huge glass that he drank and drank and drank from; I'd thought it was water but it was wine.

I turned my back on him. When he was alive, he'd been my hero, my Elvis, and then I felt ashamed of him. When he died at thirty-six years old, I was ashamed of myself for never helping him. I still am.

When my little sister later fell under the sway of alcoholism and drug addiction, I tried to help her but it didn't take. Like all of us, she's still trying to find the path back "home."

My parents never spoke of Larry's death, as though they'd closed the book on it. My father, I believe, had the death certificate changed to say Larry died of pneumonia, he was so ashamed of what had truly killed his son. And there was my father's mantra: "Don't celebrate, they'll take it away from you." They took Larry from him. Larry was such a good son.

My mother was horrible to Larry's wife and children—they became outcasts. The last time Larry tried to see my parents, they closed the door on him. Some fool had told them that if he came over for a drink, they should shut the door in his face. They did as they were told. He died three months later, leaving his young children fatherless.

My father "closed up shop," as they say, filled with self-recrimination until leukemia caught up to him. My father spent the last year of his life in and out of the hospital. My mother seldom went to see him. She sent me. When it was clear that he was near the end, they sent him home so he could die in his own bed. A nurse came daily to give him morphine; after the final shot, Barney sailed away.

My mother had spent a fortune on these gold-monogrammed hand towels that hung in the bathroom. When my father's doctor came to the house to see him the final time, the doctor wiped his hands on those towels. My mother came to my room and I thought she was about to share her sorrow with me, but this is what she whispered: "Tell him not to use the towels." Her husband was dying. Her son was dead. Her daughter was gone. She'd cut ties with her family. She had no one. Just me and the towels.

I thought I would be free after my father died. My mother was living in Walnut Creek, California, and I was hundreds of miles to the south in Los Angeles. It was what I had wanted my whole life—distance from her. But I had promised my father that I would at least play the dutiful son, so I still checked in from time to time.

I took her for an early-bird dinner not long after my father died. We were getting on rather well, both of us pretending we liked each other. And then she whispered drunkenly to me, "Take me home."

"What?"

"Take me home."

"What? Why?"

"Just do what I tell you. I've shit myself."

She invited me and Katie, my wife at the time, for the first Thanksgiving she was alone, and I agreed to go. I invited my friend Rick Podell and his girlfriend to join us. The four of us stayed safely away in a hotel, but at the appointed time we went over to my mother's house for Thanksgiving dinner. When we arrived, the table was set, and the smell of things cooking permeated the house. There were mashed potatoes and vegetables and all the expected sides. But no turkey.

"I forgot to turn on the oven," she said.

So we decided we'd eat around it and wait for the turkey to be done. A little strange, but okay.

Then she excused herself from the table and went into her bedroom. A few minutes later, while my friends and my wife and I were still sitting at the table not-eating turkey, my mother walked by the open doorway to the hall. She was completely naked from her underpants up and carrying the dress she had been wearing to the laundry room. Rick and I looked at each other and began to laugh so hard that tears spilled down our cheeks. A moment later, my mother walked back to her bedroom and closed the door. She never looked at us, and she didn't come back out. She had no idea we were there. We stopped laughing.

We turned off the oven and put everything away, and we left. It was the strangest evening I have ever experienced, and it was never spoken of again.

A few months afterward, I got a call from my business manager. "Your mother has sold the house."

"What?"

"She wants to move to L.A."

It made no sense. But my business manager found an apartment for her and made the arrangements for her move. And then there she was, alone. No friends, no one to visit her. She knew no one in the building. She didn't have a dog or a cat. She had nothing. Okay, that's not entirely true. She had one friend—well, a steady and reliable acquaintance— the delivery man from the liquor store around the corner on Robertson Boulevard.

I would visit once in a while. She had a TV blaring in every room. It was deafening. It was impossible to talk. It was its own circle of hell.

She came to visit me at work just once that I remember, when I was doing a TV show called **Mr. Sunshine,** which was produced by my friend Henry Winkler. I had the lead role, Paul Stark, who was a blind professor. It lasted just eleven episodes— they put it up against **Dynasty,** my first welcome-to-network strategy. My mother came to a taping one evening and sat in the audience. While I was changing my clothes just offstage in preparation for the taping, I could hear the warm-up guy doing his patter out front. Someone in the audience was answering back to everything he was saying, and she—it was a she—was getting big laughs. **Oh my God, it's my mother. My mother is heckling the warm-up man.**

The night before she died (nearly two decades after my father), the hospital in Century City called my assistant to fetch me out of my acting class. I excused myself to say my final good-bye. She was morphined up, basically in a coma, all but gone. I stood by her bed. Her hair was perfectly done. I kept touching it; the hairspray made it bounce back against my hand. **How do you get your hair done in ICU?** She always had her hair done three times a week, and even now, when she was ready to go, it was just so.

And here was another bit of proof of God's irony: A few years later, I was doing a series for NBC called **Bent.** My character, the dad of the family, was going through a health crisis and had to be hospitalized. The locations manager found a suitable space in the very same hospital. The hospital was no longer practical, so it was being leased out to film crews. I found myself in the same ICU ward, different bed.

When my mom died, I was dating my then-girlfriend-now-wife Kasia, and the two of us went to my mother's apartment to clean it out. She had very few things, some beauty products, a few photos. Everything there—her faux gold, her clothing, her perfume, her handbags—added up to less than a student has in a college dormitory.

It wasn't until years after she died that I opened the bag we had put her jewelry in with thoughts of dividing it up to give to the family. The smell of her perfume and just a hint of Lysol wafted out of that bag and punched me in the face. There was just no escape.

You're a piece of shit. You've always been a piece of shit. You'll always be a piece of shit.

And remember, Stinky, don't celebrate, don't say anything. Shhhh. Shhhhhh. They'll take it away from you. Oh, and your mother is very nervous.

## 5

## Sealed Orders

The world is full of people who have stopped listening to themselves or have listened only to their neighbors to learn what they ought to do, how they ought to behave, and what the values are they should be living for. You

**owe it to yourself to get on with what you're
here for.**

—JOSEPH CAMPBELL

On your mark . . . get set . . . eye roll. I have
a theory that we come into this world
with a set of sealed orders. It's not just our
physical DNA, but a sort of spiritual DNA. You
could call it your purpose or your groove or whatever word you like. Joseph Campbell called it bliss.
George Saunders, my literary "crush," calls it "one's
primary reason." Whatever you call it, it's your obligation to yourself to find it. It's not a whim, nor
a wish, but a need. It wakes you up each morning
with almost a sickness in your stomach to get on
with it. Campbell named it "the call," which I think
is so apt. It's like the phone call in the night—it's
ominous, but you have to pick it up to hear the
news; woe betide anyone who doesn't answer this
particular call.

This was mine, way before cell phones.

When I was ten years old and living in a place
called Parkmerced Apartment Towers, I could walk
out my back door up to Holloway Avenue, then
turn right twice, and there was San Francisco
State College. One day I took that walk to campus with no special intention, but an unnamed urge
pushed me on, telling me to go, that something
important was waiting for me and I needed to go
find it. (A similar urge would push me out of my

apartment in New York City in the days leading up to me meeting my wife, Kasia. More on that later.)

I saw a building with double glass doors. I walked over, opened the doors, and went inside. I walked down a linoleum-tiled hallway, passing little rooms with rows of bright lights and mirrors, not understanding what they were. I thought they were small closets. Later, I would learn they were dressing rooms. At the end of the hallway, I came out into the lobby of a little theater aptly named the Little Theater. I opened the door to the darkened theater and heard people talking loudly and in a strange way. I looked down ten rows of seats to the stage, on which were what appeared to be two old men in military uniforms of some kind. Then they stopped talking in that strange way, and talked in a normal way. Then they returned to the strange way, and what they said and did seemed to improve. They stopped, talked some more, redid the scene, and it improved again. I was mesmerized. **If you stopped and talked about it, you could fix it and it would look and sound better.** That was better than life, or at least my life.

I didn't realize it was a play; I thought they were in some altered state. I certainly was while watching. I immediately grasped the warmth in how they talked to each other, the respect and honor in their communication, like nothing I'd ever heard before. We never talked in that tone at home.

I took this strange walk every day after school. It was as if I had no choice. Every day, I'd get home, put my books down, and go to the Little Theater. My parents had no idea where I was—it was my big secret. Eventually I learned that I was watching an acting class, and two elderly men were rehearsing a scene from the Lillian Hellman play **Watch on the Rhine**. The old men were probably eighteen years old.

I started moving up the rows, getting closer to the stage. The actors started to expect me. After days of this, I got right up to the front row and they acknowledged me. "Hey, kid, how are you?" I was so in love with these people and what they were doing. As far as I was concerned, they were heroes.

One day they stopped the scene to talk through a problem. "What do you think, kid?" They were asking **me** what I thought? I told them, and, get this, they incorporated what I said into the action. I assume it was just to be polite to this strange kid who showed up every day with his apple and bag of potato chips, but they tried out my suggestion, and it worked. Connection. I had made a connection. No one had ever asked my opinion before, ever.

When they were done with their final rehearsal before presenting the scene in class the next day, they invited me onstage to help them strike the set.

I had no idea what "strike the set" meant. (It means clear the stage.) "Grab that rock, will you?"

There were stairs at either end of the stage. I left my seat and walked up the right staircase, and then I was standing on a stage for the first time in my life. The stage boards were sturdy and the lights from above and the footlights (yes, there were footlights) made it warm and comfortable. It was different up there. I looked at the student actors, the theater drapes, the empty seats out in the audience, and something started to make sense. I crossed to the boulder and I thought they were goofing on me. "I'm not going to be able to lift this," I said.

"Go ahead, kid. You can lift it."

I leaned down and put my arms around this boulder, ready to put all my strength into hoisting it. To my shock, I lifted it effortlessly—it was made of celastic, a form of plastic—and I raised it over my head.

This was me running around in my new Keds.

This was me picking the winners at the Soap Box Derby.

This was the **itzrach ben baruch** of my bar mitzvah.

This was Jeffrey Michael, son of Barney and Eileen, wearing the red bowtie my grandma Gertrude Salzberg from Kiev, Ukraine, had given me.

I burst into tears, and then I laughed. **Yes.**

The actors stood there, as witness.
**Yes.**
It was everything. It was right. It was good. **Yes.**
**This—yes—this.**
**Please, please make it go on forever.**
I was ten years old, and I was home.

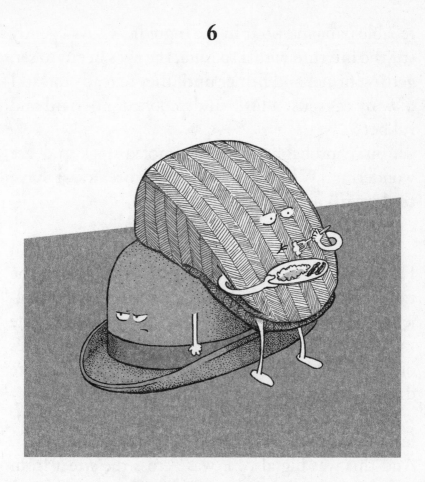

## 6

## Scrambled Eggs

Every Saturday morning, I make scrambled eggs for my kids Hugo, Eli, Gabriel, and Evie. What can I say, they like my eggs. The kids help me put eggs, a little milk, some parsley, pepper, and truffle salt into a bowl. I heat the old reliable pan, and pour in the ingredients. As I gently stir the mixture with a spatula, the eggs begin to set, getting firmer and firmer until they're ready to eat. I like my eggs just a little undercooked, not hard and rubbery.

You've probably made scrambled eggs and are wondering, **What the fuck does breakfast have to do with acting?**

Bear with me.

After walking over to the Little Theater at San Francisco State nearly every afternoon from the time I was ten, it made sense to me to go to college there when the time came. I could have gone to Berkeley, maybe Stanford, or a couple of colleges out East, but by then I had learned that the SF State drama department was fantastic, and the faculty wise and practical. They were all steeped in professional theater with big résumés and credentials. And this was big also: it was across the street from where I already lived with my family, so I could save money by continuing to live at home. I think my staying close pleased my father, but not as much as the $48-per-semester price tag, which was a result of Governor Pat Brown's mandate that every person in California who wanted to go to college should be able to go.

(In 2009, I was named Alumnus of the Year at the graduation ceremony where baseball legend Willie Mays was giving the commencement address. As I sat there in cap and gown—**That's Willie Mays. I'm** sitting with Willie Mays. #24. THE "SAY HEY" KID—I could literally see the apartment complex the Tambors lived in: Apt. 2K, 14 Gonzalez Drive to my left, and 14 Vidal Drive to my right.)

Jack Cook was a body movement teacher and a huge advocate of mime; he'd studied with Jacques Lecoq in Paris. He was also a director, and took on one show every year. During my freshman year, he cast me in my very first role in my very first show, as Victor the butler in **Gigi.** When I saw my name on the casting board next to the theater, I screamed out loud.

Jack's approach to directing was revolutionary to me, and stays with me to this day. At first, in my ignorance, I thought it was laziness, but it was actually theater smarts from a man who knew exactly what it took to get the very best from his actors and make a superior production. He was a no-bullshit guy, and he believed in me from the day I walked into that building at 1600 Holloway Drive. Maybe I was still wearing the aura of the ten-year-old kid who used to walk the halls of that very theater department.

The following are life lessons from Jack Cook:

## LESSON #1: THE HAT

He would say, "You're doing great," and then give you a note that sometimes could be a little tough. And we took it because he'd given us confidence first. I was doing a show called **Mr. Dandyweather's Holiday,** and during a run-through I got a little careless and added some superfluous moves and gestures in an effort to make what was already funny funnier. Jack took me aside and said, "You're good with what we've been doing. You don't need to put a hat on a hat." He was saying: If you comment on it, you kill it. If there's a hat already on your head, why in God's name would you put another hat on top of it? The audience doesn't like to see you wink.

(When I'm working with the great Marie Schley, the brilliant costumer for **Transparent,** to build a look for Maura, we often look at each other in the mirror and say, "Mmmm, hat?" And we keep looking for the right outfit.)

## LESSON #2: OFF BOOK

Jack was adamant about this one: You must come to the first rehearsal off book—with your lines memorized. Besides being awfully arbitrary, this was the '60s, the days of the Method and Stanislavski, Sanford Meisner this and Lee Strasberg that. Memorizing your lines was bush league, we thought, amateur stuff. Jack was leaving no room for "process," we complained. **This isn't artistic! This is bullshit!**

But the truth was, Jack's shows were always better-honed and better-prepared. His actors luxuriated in preparedness, which gave them—me—confidence.

This very note came shining through when I was doing David Mamet's **Glengarry Glen Ross** on Broadway. The great William H. Macy, a Mamet veteran, when asked what one should expect he said, "Learn your lines before."

David is the genius of geniuses and the friend of friends, and the peach of peaches. (I have to say that, because he once left a message calling me "cupcake," so I must return the serve—hi, David.) But he can be a hard taskmaster when it comes to dialogue. He writes lines where "the" is sometimes just "th." But it is all there in the line. His genius is that he puts subtext **in** the text, much like Shakespeare. No, exactly like Shakespeare. The action is in the text. Learn it and you're on your way.

I love that phrase, "on your way." The director Andrea Arnold says "On your way" instead of "Action." Instead of "Cut," she says "Thank you."

It's gorgeous, I love it. What a world, that has directors like Andrea Arnold in it. Hi, Andrea.

This is what Jack knew, that forcing us to confront the text made us get ready in thought and
character. We had begun the process. We weren't
waiting for his direction. We were co-creators. It
wasn't about learning the lines, it was about learning the part.

## LESSON #3: THE KICKER

About two weeks into the four- or five-week rehearsal period, Jack would leave. Let me repeat: the
director would leave. For a week.

We were blocked, which means we had all the
stage movement learned, and were up on our feet.
He'd say, "Okay, see you in a week. Start running
it." That's it. No advice, no notes. Not even a wave at
the door. We would rehearse with the stage manager while he was gone.

I've never seen any other director do this, but it
worked extremely well for him. He believed in his
cast, and he believed in the play, and he believed in
his process.

When Jack walked away, he'd assembled the ingredients and started the cooking, just the way I
make scrambled eggs. (You thought I forgot about
the eggs, didn't you?) By leaving us to it, he was al-
lowing the actors the time and space for our perfor-

mances to come to that flash point. In this brilliant way, his "lack of direction" **was** direction. He was telling us, "You've got this. You're ready to go. Just let it come together."

When he came back, the show was on its legs. It was strong and had a core and a heart and had indeed improved and even changed. He would re-embrace it and take it on home to the audience. The only reason we could do that is he gave us such confidence. He taught me to seek out other mentors in my life and career who would also give me confidence. I took that to heart. I would always seek out collaborators who gave me confidence.

**CUT TO:** Filming Season Three of **Transparent.** I was doing a tough scene, and I found myself flailing. I was working opposite Jenny O'Hara, who plays Maura's sister, Bryna. She's a brilliant actress, and in the scene her character is a couple of sheets to the wind, and suddenly I'm reminded of my mother, and it was throwing me. I was "getting a little on me," as they say. The scene was hurting me. I was losing words, which I never do. Then the legendary and saintly Anjelica Huston took me aside and said, "You're brilliant. Don't be so hard on yourself. You can't miss here." And I was fine for the rest of the night of shooting. Anjelica had read that I was struggling with the subject matter and she stepped in and gave me my confidence back. She "got" me.

You have to work with people who give you confidence. You just do. Hi, Anjelica.

Oh, one more thing about Jack Cook, and this may be the ultimate lesson of all. In early 2011, nearly five decades after I'd been his student, I called him. I found his number in the San Francisco directory and decided to give it a shot. **Ring. Ring. Ring.**

"Hello?"

It was Jack, a little raspier, a little lower in timbre, but it was Jack. We talked for about half an hour, remembering this, not remembering that. He told me his lovely partner, William Browder, was no longer alive.

Before we said good-bye, I said, "Jack, thank you. There are no adequate words, but you changed everything. Is there anything I can do for you?"

After a pause, he gave me this last lesson: "Call back."

Jack Cook, the man who taught me freedom and

confidence, died a few weeks later. He was eighty-nine years old. His obituary in the **San Francisco Chronicle** noted, "He is survived by dozens of talented and successful students."

Good-bye, Jack Cook. Thank you.

## 7

## Troubadour

When I go to the theater and the lights dim, and there's that second alone in the complete darkness, I tear up. I'm not quite sure what it is, maybe that hush of expectancy, of intimacy, of connection; it is the sacred pact between audience and performer. It is what E. M. Forster was thinking when he wrote in **Howards End**: "Connect. Only connect." For me, it is the red bowtie.

It happened again last night. I went to see my lovely friend Judith Light at the Lucille Lortel Theatre in New York on the opening night of Neil LaBute's one-woman play **All the Ways to Say I Love You.** The audience was talking, then the house lights dimmed halfway, the audience hushed, and then complete darkness. In that silence, we are together, we hope, we need. There's apprehension. It's not relaxed, that silence. It's full of need— **Please, please, let this be the message that I need, that changes me for the better or at least gets me through the night.** Then the curtain rose, and the show began. Judith killed. This is why they invented the phrase "artistic killer." There was not a heart left unbroken, especially mine.

Like me, Judith got her start in repertory theater, and repertory theater is not for the faint of heart. We all had to earn the right to be there.

In 1965, I graduated from San Francisco State summa cum laude, which all of you who studied Latin know means I had one of the larger laudes in my graduating class. From there I moved to Detroit, Michigan, to attend graduate school at Wayne State University. I love Detroit. It has one of the best art institutes in the world, the best Greek food in "Greek town," the Tigers are mighty and the

Lions are fantastic, and Wayne is one of the best universities going. If your doctor or your lawyer is from Wayne State, you're going to live and/or win your lawsuit.

But I thought all cities were like San Francisco. Detroit is not like San Francisco. Downtown Detroit, where I lived on Cass and Hancock, was especially not like San Francisco. It was inner city and had fallen on hard times. Around campus, it was très funky. Right across the street from the Hilberry Classic Theatre, there was Teddy's, where grease was on and in the menu, the coffee was burnt and as acidic as Teddy's face when anyone entered. The diner was the prototype of the Aykroyd/Belushi "cheeseburger, cheeseburger" sketch from early **SNL**.

My life at Wayne State was all theater all the time. In the mornings, I attended graduate classes and I also taught speech, theater, and acting classes to undergraduates. Afternoons between 1:00 p.m. and 5:00 p.m. were for rehearsal, a break for dinner until 7:00 p.m., and back to the Hilberry for performances. Theater students participated in real repertory theater, real meaning a different play every night. We would do **The Tempest** one night, **Twelfth Night** the next, John Whiting's **The Devils** the next, and a Restoration comedy the next. I did a lot of Feydeau farces. I still have nightmares about making my entrance onstage and having no idea what play we were doing.

My first-ever review was of my Caliban in **The Tempest,** of which the critic Jay Carr wrote in the **Detroit News:** "Jeffrey Tambor is a beaded bag gone wrong." They weren't wrong about the beads— I was covered with green makeup and shiny beads. It was way wrong. I even chewed a pack of chlorophyll gum to turn my tongue green before my entrance, and I would dart it out during every speech. It was reptilian and stupid; such was my waywardness.

The thing about repertory theater is that the play goes on even if it's not ready. My study of acting went straight from theory to **Oh my God, these people have paid money, and I have no idea what the fuck I'm doing.** The season begins in September and runs through May, so you build the show in front of the audience. For example, our production of Shakespeare's **Twelfth Night,** in which I played Sir Andrew Aguecheek, opened to so-so reviews, but by the spring it had become one of the strongest, and most delightful, productions I was ever in.

During my third year of graduate school, I decided to audition for the TCGs. The Theatre Communications Group is the umbrella organization for resident theaters all over the country. And repertory theater was a growing and exciting part of the national theater scene, with new theaters being founded by esteemed artists from coast to coast. William Ball founded the American Conservatory Theater in San Francisco in 1965; David Wheeler founded the Theatre Company of Boston in 1963;

Gordon Davidson started the Mark Taper Forum in Los Angeles in 1967. What you hoped to walk away with was a LORT contract. The League of Resident Theatres administers contracts between the regional theaters and the Actors' Equity Association, and you could become either an apprentice or a full-fledged resident actor.

You were required to prepare a four-minute audition: two minutes of something classical, and two minutes of something modern. I chose Tyrone from **Long Day's Journey into Night** and **Falstaff.** There were several levels of auditions to get through—local, regional, state—before you were invited to the national audition held every year in Chicago.

I made it through the preliminaries and booked myself a room at the Statler Hilton on Michigan Avenue overlooking Lake Michigan. On the morning of the audition, I walked the few blocks from the hotel to the 11th Street Theater. There was a table in the lobby where auditioning actors were to sign in.

"We're going in alphabetical order, so come back around three o'clock," the woman at the desk told me.

I went back to my room to warm up and prepare. At the appointed time, I returned to the theater, which was packed with the artistic directors of nearly every theater in the country. This audition in front of this room is arguably the most important and prestigious audition of a young actor's career.

I did my Falstaff and my Tyrone. It went okay. Not great. Okay. I was told to come back after lunch, when I could check my box to see which ADs wanted to see me. I think I had three or four, at most.

One of the people was David Wheeler of the Theatre Company of Boston, who was, as they say, a BFD. He essentially turned Boston into a theater town. When I met with him, he said, "Now, listen to me. You're a good actor. You did well. But I have people who are sixty-five to play Falstaff. You're twenty-five. Choose material that is better for you."

"So, you're not interested in me?" I said.

"I have no place for you."

"So . . . no."

"I have no place for you."

"So—you're not offering me a position?"

"Choose better material."

"So . . . ?"

I went back to Detroit and my classes and repertory at the Hilberry Classic Theatre.

A year later I tried again. Two minutes of Bertolt Brecht's **Edward II** and two minutes of Anton Chekhov's **The Boor.** With Jack Cook's lesson about preparation implanted deep in my brain, I worked on my audition for six months. I thought that was my problem the first time, that I hadn't prepared enough, never mind that David Wheeler had told me I simply picked the wrong material. I didn't hear it. I'm the student who underlined every line in the textbook so when it was time to study for the test, I had to read the whole thing again cover to cover, and I was no less overzealous in my preparation now. I would do my audition for everyone I knew, whether they wanted to see it or not. I did it for strangers. If someone passing on the street happened to make eye contact, I did it for them. I did it over and over and over and over, ad nauseam, until I had that thing **down.**

I went to the local audition, got accepted. I went to the regional audition, got accepted. I went to the state audition, got accepted. I was heading back to Chicago.

Once again, I got a room at the Statler Hilton. This time I brought my wife, Joyce. We went for dinner the evening before. And then I spent the rest of the night unable to sleep, going over and over the audition in my head. There was so much riding on this—it was the audition of my life.

In the morning, I took the now-familiar walk to the 11th Street Theater to sign in before returning to the hotel to do my prep routine: work out, do yoga, worry, smoke cigarettes, worry, have a shower and shave while worrying, and warm up.

"Okay, I'll see you later," I said after I signed in.

"Where are you going? We're reversing the order this year. We're going from Z to A. You're up now."

**What? Fuck.**

There was one person before me, Zbrinski or somebody, and then it was my turn. I walked down to the stage, up the side stairs, stepped to the center, and looked out at all of those ADs who held my future in their hands. I opened my mouth and began.

Because I had rehearsed so much in the months leading up to this moment, it was like automatic writing. The words just flowed from me. I did **Edward II** first. It was okay. Then I turned my back to the audience for a moment, then back around to face them and said my first line from **The Boor:** "You have no idea how to treat a lady, Mr. Smirnov." It got a huge laugh. Then my next line got a huge laugh. And the next. I sailed.

I walked off the stage in complete silence, but the casting director and producer Rosemarie Tichler, who went on to become the casting doyenne of New York City and Joseph Papp's Shakespeare Festival, stopped me on the way out and said, "Have a nice lunch. You're going to be a very busy man this afternoon." And indeed, that afternoon I received offers from the Seattle Repertory Theatre, Milwaukee Repertory Theater, Actors Theatre of Louisville, Asolo Repertory Theatre, Provincetown Theater, San Diego Repertory Theatre, almost every theater in the country (except the Theatre Company of Boston—neither David Wheeler nor any of his people were in attendance that year). I would work for the next eight to ten years off that one four-minute audition.

That audition was about being in the moment. It was about risk, and play, and spontaneity. Yes, I had prepared, but in the moment I'd had to trust the preparation and just let it come. It was there, it had always been there, just waiting to be asked to the dance. **That** was why it worked. I would forget this lesson and have to learn it again and again in the course of my career. But for those four minutes, it didn't matter that I was dressed badly and unshaven, because apparently I was wearing this rather big red bowtie.

My first gig was at the Seattle Rep. Joyce and I sold our red Volkswagen for $300 (I cried) and bought a Greenbrier station wagon (green) so we could fit our two cats, Andrew and Buster, and our tchotchkes, and we headed west. We rented an apartment in the back of a house on Queen Anne Hill that overlooked the entire city. Our landlord was an Amway salesman, and he charged us $125 a month.

Seattle was perfect for me. As Ken Kesey famously said, to understand madness, you have to spend a winter in the Pacific Northwest. It was foggy and rainy all the time. It suited my personality. My people understand this place.

My very first role was Senator Logan in Arthur Kopit's **Indians,** directed by Arne Zaslove; the cast included Manu Tupou, who had been in the Broadway production of the play a few years earlier. The acting staff was largely composed of young actors and students from the University of Washington. It was culture shock in so many ways, not least of which was having free time. In Detroit, the hours of my days were crammed with class and teaching and rehearsals and performances. Now, I would go to rehearsal, do the few scenes I had, and the director would say, "Okay, you're done for the day." I had no idea what to do with my life. It was a shock.

It was even worse when I was only understudying. When you understudy, you might as well have a sign around your neck that says DEATH / PLAGUE, because you only go on if someone gets sick. I understudied one actor who was such an asshole, he would come to my dressing room door, throw it open, scream, "I'm never going to get sick, goddammit!" and slam the door shut.

So I started baking bread. I'd go to the famed Pike Place Market every day and buy the ingredients, and I'd bake loaves and loaves of French bread and take them to the theater, although there was something about the weather there—maybe it was that the barometric pressure was always low because of the rain—the bread wouldn't rise.

The theater was right next to the Seattle Sonics arena, so on nights when there were home games, I would check in at the theater: "He's here. You're free for the evening." I would go over there, sneak in, grab a seat in the first row, and watch basketball and munch on my unleavened French bread. I knew every move in the Sonics playbook.

It was the beginning of a great adventure, traveling in that old station wagon with Joyce and the cats, going from town to town like troubadours of old who went from village to village, were invited in for a bite to eat, and in exchange entertained their host. We rented cheap apartments, sometimes in beautiful neighborhoods, and led a simple life. This is what acting was to me, and I loved it.

We ended up staying in Milwaukee for five years. Milwaukee was a revelation: I didn't know that when it was ten below in the dead of January, people went on about their lives as though nothing remarkable was occurring. I would be at the theater before a show, thinking, **We can't possibly perform tonight, there's a blizzard!** And the place would be packed, night after night. It was at the Milwaukee Rep that I met Judith Light in 1971, more than forty years before we would costar in **Transparent.** We still have a running argument about whether she forgot to introduce me onstage one night by forgetting the cue line. She denies; **j'accuse.** She can rebut in **her** book.

I want to be very clear about the caliber of actors who worked in repertory theater. These were not lesser actors. I shared a dressing room for a year in Milwaukee with an actor named Bill McKerrigan. We spent so much time together, we became like family. We talked about life, we shared recipes, we told jokes, we fought. Bill wasn't passing through Milwaukee; he really lived there. He brought up his kids in Milwaukee. And he was one of the finest actors I've ever worked with. He didn't want to do all the red carpet horseshit, he just wanted to act. Like so many actors I encountered during those years traveling the country, he was a dedicated artist. We all were.

Actors like Bill were citizens of whatever city they were in; they paid taxes there; they voted there; they had library cards there. And there are still actors like that all over the country. There are actors in those local companies who kill in show after show, and they never leave because they are already doing exactly what they want to do.

It was in these theaters that I learned how to act for real. We did six shows a week—with two on Saturday, at 4:15 and 8:15—while rehearsing the next show in the rotation. The work was amazing, the plays were amazing, and everybody was completely invested.

There were two newspapers in town—the **Sentinel** in the morning and the **Journal** in the afternoon—and on the Saturday after opening night, when the reviews came out, the good ones were posted in a frame backstage. Some Saturdays, there were two reviews in those frames. Some Saturdays, there was just one. And some Saturdays, the frames remained empty. That was life at the Milwaukee Rep.

One winter, the Rep, as we called it, did a Midwest tour of Molière's **The School for Wives.** The production was directed by the theater's genius artistic director, Nagle Jackson, the man who lured me to Milwaukee from San Diego Rep, where we did **The Taming of the Shrew** together.

On the tour, I played Arnolphe, one of Molière's biggest and most outrageous fools. I had decided to quit smoking the day of our first run-through, because I realized that I would need to be in shape for the tour. At the end of the day, Nagle gave various cast members notes, and sent them on their way. He didn't give me a single note, but he asked me to stay back for a minute after he'd dismissed the others. He complimented my handling of the material and Richard Wilbur's rhyming verse translation, my characterization, my movement. "I have just one note," he said.

"Yes?"

"Can you start playing with the rest of the cast?"

I gathered my things, my script, my winter coat and hat, and went directly to the corner store to buy a carton of cigarettes. He'd caught me performing up my own ass, and I am forever grateful to him. It is one of the finest notes I have ever received. Thanks, Nagle.

When the show was on its feet, we hit the road. Our first night was in a packed gymnasium in Spearfish, South Dakota; the laughs were huge and the welcome gigantic. The audience was so grateful and appreciative of this classical comedy we brought them. In some towns, where there were no restaurants to speak of, we were invited into people's homes for dinner before the show. The next morning, it was back on the bus to Ames, Iowa, or Duluth, Minnesota, where we were picked up again and taken to dinner before the performance. Our final stop on the tour was the John Deere Tractor Center in Moline, Illinois; the cast dressed downstairs with the tractors.

At every stop, people came out in droves to see the show and stayed to talk to the cast afterward. There were invitations after the show for pie and coffee. We learned about these wonderful people and their communities. They needed the theater, they needed us. This wasn't entertainment, it was vital, and we were welcomed into their lives. This was true theater and true connection, authentic and humble. Not a red carpet in sight.

We repertory actors were perhaps a bit overinvested—we were derisive of actors who appeared on television or did commercials. We didn't even watch television. We were onstage! I was onstage when the Detroit Tigers won the 1968 World Series and the audience and crew started clapping because they could hear the cheering and hooting outside the theater. I was in rehearsal when the moon landing happened, and someone suggested we take a break and watch on a TV in the lobby. When another actor told us about a television job they got, we snickered. When Laurence Olivier did his one and only television commercial for a Polaroid camera in 1972, painstakingly describing how to load the film, we thought the world had ended.

Incidentally, a few years later, after I had started to appear regularly on shows like **Kojak** and **M\*A\*S\*H,** I was at a Lakers game in Los Angeles sitting high up in the arena.

A guy sitting near me said, "Hey, you're on television, right?"

"Yeah, I am."

"You like the Lakers?"

"I love the Lakers."

Then he looked down courtside and back up at me, then back down courtside. "Oh, I get it. Film down there, television up here."

It was as if I'd said it, because it was exactly what I thought.

After five years in Milwaukee, I journeyed south of the Mason–Dixon Line. I had the worst review of my life—and the best review of my life—in Louisville, Kentucky. I was at the Actors Theatre playing Tartuffe as though I were the hottest piece of shit that ever came down the mountainside. I preened and pranced around the stage—**Look at me! Look at me!** It was admittedly a lapse in taste, and the reviewer for the **Louisville Courier,** William Mootz, one of the deans of American criticism, called me on it. The morning after the show opened, I woke up and went to the kitchen to check out the review in the newspaper. There was no paper, just my wife standing by the sink in her blue bathrobe.

"Where's the paper?" I asked.

"It didn't come today," Joyce said.

"The **Louisville Courier** didn't come today?"

"Nope."

That's when I noticed a suspicious bulge under her robe.

"Let me see it," I said.

"Oh, honey. Honey, don't."

I held my hand out until she caved and withdrew the folded Arts and Leisure section.

It remains to date the most excoriating review I have ever received. He described my performance as "Groucho Marx uneasily in search of a gag by George S. Kaufman." It wasn't just a bad review, it was a how-dare-you review. "Tambor destroys **Tartuffe** by playing the central character as if he were a mindless buffoon." I burst into tears after reading it. It felt like somebody had caught me out. I was devastated.

Here's the thing about bad reviews: no one calls you when you get one. You get calls when you get good reviews. You get calls when you get 98% on Rotten Tomatoes. You get calls when someone dies.

And the worst part is, you still have to go to work and do it again.

You go to the theater, and you walk past the silent stage manager who doesn't look you in the eye. You go to your dressing room and close the door.

**Knock knock knock.**

"Come in."

"Ohhhh. I'm **so** sorry."

"I'm fine. I'm fine."

"I just want to tell you that I think you're very good in this show."

"Okay, thank you. See you onstage."

**Knock knock knock.**

"Come in."

"Are you okay?" The voice quavering on the edge of tears. "Are you going to be all right?"

"Yes, I'm fine. I'll see you onstage."

**Knock knock knock.**

"I think you're one of the finest actors out there. Are you okay?"

On and on and on it goes. By curtain time, you want to kill yourself.

Then you go out onstage. The curtain goes up, and you realize the audience has read that review too. Every laugh you had the previous night is gone. **William Mootz is so right. That's what they're thinking.** It is the single worst experience, and every actor has to go through it.

A month later, Mr. Mootz reviewed me again. I was directing the stage adaptation of **One Flew**

**Over the Cuckoo's Nest,** and this time the word "triumph" was in the headline. The performance had received a standing ovation at the first intermission. I was a hero. And the calls came in. My takeaway was that, ever after, I would always make the call when someone got a lousy review.

That production was notable for one other thing. During the rehearsal phase a few weeks earlier, Joyce had said to me over breakfast as I was heading out the door, "I think I missed a period." I was busy rehearsing for **Tartuffe,** so I didn't have time to talk to her about it, but I knew I'd see her later in the day when I went to the performance of **Cuckoo's Nest,** since she was playing one of the nurses and I was planning to give the cast some notes.

When I got there, Joyce was onstage with the actor G. W. Bailey, who was playing one of the patients, named Cheswick. In the scene, Cheswick is taunting the nurse, and the line she is supposed to say is something like "Don't touch me! I'm a nurse!" But as I'm sitting in the back of the house watching, and I guess because it was on her mind, I heard Joyce say, "Don't touch me! I'm pregnant!" We would be back in Milwaukee when our daughter, Molly, was born about seven months later.

Maybe six months after that day in Louisville, I was sitting in the dark offstage in Milwaukee, waiting for my scene in our production of Brecht's **The Visions of Simone Machard,** when it hit me. **I have to go to New York. I have to try it.** I was thirty-two years old, and I'd been doing regional theater for a decade. I went home that night and told Joyce. That weekend, we sold all of our books. Weeks later, I gave notice. The artistic director had become a friend by then, but he understood my going. I left Joyce and our infant daughter Molly in Milwaukee with a promise to find an apartment and send for them.

One of my former cast mates, Charlie Kimbrough, had made the move east some time earlier and had become a successful Broadway actor. I called him, and asked if he could introduce me to his agent, Milton Goldman at ICM, who was one of the most powerful in the business. He agreed and offered me his guest room in Dobbs Ferry in Westchester County, about thirty minutes north of the city.

I flew in during a blizzard, but Charlie met me at the airport and drove me up to his house. We had a lovely dinner and I hit the hay.

The following morning at breakfast, Charlie said, "I don't know if I can do it." He was getting cold feet about introducing me to Milton.

"You have to. It's why I'm here."

I finally persuaded him to make the call and get me an appointment. I took the train into Grand Central later that day.

When I arrived in Milton's office, he had two phones working at the same time, one to each ear. In one was the composer Gian Carlo Menotti (**Amahl and the Night Visitors**), and in the other was Vincent Price. To this day, I have no idea why these two would be communicating through Mr. Goldman or about what. While he carried on his conversations, I looked at the books on his shelves. I wasn't as nervous as I thought I would be. When he got off the phones, we talked for a bit, and then he sent me to meet with another agent, Doris Mantz, who booked commercials. In the mid-'70s, there were lots of commercials that featured beleaguered, balding young fathers. There was a well-known actor named Ken Kimmins who had done a lot of these commercials, but he had recently left the agency. When I met with Doris, her eyes were virtually feasting on me. That's right, I was balding and Ken Kimmins had just left. (Hi, Ken! Thanks, Ken!)

Doris then called Sheila Robinson, a theatrical agent whose clients included Meryl Streep, and told her, "Don't let him leave the building." I then met with Sheila and she said, "I'll take care of you," and I was signed.

That night, I didn't go back to Dobbs Ferry. A composer friend from Milwaukee had a small apartment on the East Side of Manhattan, and he offered it to me while he was out of town. The taxi left me off in front of the building, and I walked up the stairs to the second floor. I opened the door and thought, **What a lovely black carpet. Wait, that's—** The carpet was moving. **What the fuck is that? Oh my God, those are cockroaches.** He never mentioned the 730,000 roommates I'd have.

My upstairs neighbor was the fabulous Judith Light, who had made the move to New York before me. That night, Judith and her friend Warner Shook took me to see Bobby Short at the Carlyle Hotel. It was magical, my first night in New York City. I was so happy. Judith leaned over to me and said, "It won't always be like this."

For the next year, I booked commercial after commercial. My first one was shot in Cape May, New Jersey. It was my introduction to waiting around for a long time, working for the tiniest amount of time, and getting paid a lot. It completely threw me. I spent most of the time ordering room service at my hotel.

I did a National Airlines commercial. It was seven thirty in the morning on a sound stage in lower Manhattan. I was dressed in a suit to play the young bald man in business class.

The young bald businessman is watching television, he laughs. "Heh heh heh heh." He turns to the camera and he says, "National Airlines, take me, I'm yours."

"Great, we got it." It's 7:32. It's a perfect take. We're done.

When you do these commercials, the director is first rate. The costumer, first rate. The makeup artist, first rate. The ad agency, first rate.

The client said, "But we paid for the sound stage and the actor for the whole day."

"We have the commercial. You just saw it. It's perfect."

"Yes. Let's keep doing it."

"But why?"

"Because we have the actor and the sound stage."

We did another one. And another one. And another one. And another one.

Now it's 9:15.

We do another one. Another one. Another one. Until lunch.

Again, we have the commercial. All I'm doing is repeating myself. We go to lunch. The crew eats together. The client sits apart, staring straight ahead, wondering about the validity of their lives.

Then we go back. We do it again. 3:00. "National Airlines, take me, I'm yours." 4:15. We've had the commercial since 7:32. I keep saying it. "National Airlines, take me, I'm yours. National Airlines, take me, I'm yours."

The director comes over to me. "The client is a little worried about something." He was a famous commercial director in New York.

"What?"

"I don't even know how to say this. I'll just say it. It's the **k**. They think you're starting to sound a little Jewish."

"You know we have this commercial."

"Yeah, I know. Try it again."

As soon as they put that in my head, I couldn't

control myself. With each successive take, the **k** got broader and broader until I was Zero Mostel in **Fiddler on the Roof.** I couldn't control it. It is now 5:15 and we're going into overtime. People are getting a little tired. Take after take, it gets more and more Jewish. I sound like Golda Meir. Finally, I said, "I got it. I have the answer."

"What is it?"

"We're going to take out the **k.**"

"Great! Do it. Action!"

"National Airlines, tae me, I'm yours."

"Cut! Print!"

When the commercial airs, it's the first take, the 7:32 take.

I made $40,000 that first year, which was a lot of money then. I found an apartment, and Joyce and little Molly joined me. But I couldn't get arrested in the theater.

Until I got a break.

## 8

## Tambor's Big Break

"Go with the kid," Arthur Penn said during the casting of the L.A. production of **Sly Fox.** I had been an understudy for Héctor Elizondo in the Broadway production and had gone on when Héctor left the production.

The producers said, "But he doesn't have any credits" (even though I did have a credit in this very show, but never mind).

Arthur insisted. "Go with the kid." I heard him talking on the phone to Larry Gelbart, who'd written the script, saying, "Wait till you see the kid."

Actors talk about when they got their "big break" in show business. I've had more than one. In fact, there have been so many breaks, starting when I was still a kid, it's hard to pinpoint just one. The prepared but unprepared four-minute audition that led to a decade of work was one. And I'm still getting them, fifty years after I started acting. I got one in my late forties when I landed the role of Hank Kingsley on **The Larry Sanders Show.** I got another one in my late fifties: to be George and Oscar Bluth on **Arrested Development.** And I was nigh on seventy years old when Jill Soloway bestowed Maura Pfefferman of **Transparent** on me and changed my life.

But if a break is the moment when you cross the Rubicon, when the game changes, then New York in 1976 is a good place to start.

Joyce and Molly and I were living in a tiny apartment at 108 Dean Street in Brooklyn. This was not the tony, gentrified Brooklyn of today. I had the battery of my old beat-up Greenbrier station wagon stolen three times **in one day.**

I was taking the F train into Manhattan to audition for commercials, but I couldn't get a theater audition. I kept asking my agent, Sheila Robinson, what was going on, and she kept saying, "It takes time" or "You're still new, be patient." I got the sense she was placating me.

I finally got an audition for a small role in an off-Broadway production. After my reading, the casting directors said, "Where have you been? We've never heard of you."

"I've been submitted many times," I said. "I'm with ICM."

They looked through their files. They had no record of me.

And that's how I found out that it wasn't that I wasn't getting auditions; I wasn't even being offered for them. I called Sheila as soon as I got home. It turned out that Sheila had to route her audition lists through superagent Ed Limato, who was the star of ICM at the time. He'd brought Richard Gere to the firm. For some reason, Uncle Ed never wanted to send me out for anything.

Then I heard about a play that was going to be produced on Broadway, a comedy called **Sly Fox** written by Larry Gelbart of **M*A*S*H** fame. It was going to star George C. Scott, who had famously refused the Academy Award he won for **Patton** a few years earlier, and be directed by the hottest director around, Arthur Penn, who had helmed **Bonnie and Clyde,** among other masterpieces.

I confronted Sheila, and I guess she confronted

Uncle Ed, because they got me an audition with the doyenne of Broadway casting, a woman by the name of Ms. Rich. Her full name was Shirley Rich, or rather Ms. Shirley-don't-ever-call-me-Shirley Rich, as everybody warned me. And I mean everybody. My agent, my manager, her secretary said, "Don't call her Shirley!" The receptionist said, "Don't call her Shirley." I think the guy who delivered the coffee and bagels said, "You heard about the Shirley thing, right?"

I walked into her office and Ms. Rich was very gracious, asking why she'd never heard of me. We talked a little, and she seemed to sense that I was on edge. "Are you nervous, Jeffrey?"

"Not about the audition, just about calling you Shirley. Everyone told me not to."

There was a pause, and then came a big smile. We were instant friends. She interviewed me for an hour, during which we talked about everything under the sun, just me and Shirley. She was very old-school, straight out of a Damon Runyon story. She referred to an actress's legs as "gams." I loved her.

Shirley arranged for me to meet with Arthur Penn. He was not only one of the finest theater and film directors, he also taught at the Actors Studio, the famed training ground on West Forty-Fourth Street founded by Elia Kazan, Cheryl Crawford, and Robert Lewis in 1947. I would sometimes stand on the opposite sidewalk and watch the luminaries of stage and film walk into that building. This was **that** Arthur Penn, and this was **that** big chance.

And then I got a call. My older brother, Larry, my hero, had died at the age of thirty-six. I had to go to California for the funeral. Shirley had to change the date for my callback. If you can imagine what it was like to see my father bury his firstborn son, you have an idea of how that went.

When I got back to New York, I had my meeting with Mr. Penn at his office in the Gulf and Western Building on Columbus Circle. (Don't look for it; it's a Trump hotel now.) We were about to begin reading when he stopped me and said, "How are you?"

I started telling him about my brother and the funeral. We never got around to reading the scene I had prepared for. Arthur and I talked for a long time, about life and death, everything but **Sly**

**Fox.** In fact, I never did audition for the part at all. We just talked, and I walked out of there with the role.

I would make my debut on Broadway playing the part of the First Servant, and I would be the understudy for two other actors in the cast. My friends told me not to take it, that accepting an understudy role would relegate me to being an understudy for the rest of my career. You know what I thought? It was a Broadway play—Broadway!—and it starred some of the greatest actors of the day: In addition to George C. Scott, there was Jack Gilford, Trish Van Devere, Bob Dishy, Gretchen Wyler, not to mention Héctor Elizondo and John Heffernan, both of whom I'd be understudying. What am I, crazy? Of course I accepted. I used to call Héctor my "overstudy."

The First Servant had a big speech at the beginning of the play. What more could I ask for in my debut? But after the table reading, Arthur Penn walked over to me and took my script in hand, and with a red pencil he crossed through the entire speech. George C. Scott, my acting hero, was standing next to me: "The old red pencil, huh?" I ended up with three lines—or really one line said three times: "You look wonderful, sir." Those three lines, which I would repeat for the next two years, changed my career.

Eighteen months into the run, Héctor Elizondo missed a performance, so I would go on that night as Able, a huge role, and I would play opposite George C. Scott, my hero.

Before my debut performance, he came up to my dressing room—four flights up.

"Any lines you wanna run?" he asked in that gruff voice.

I said no, and continued lathering spirit gum on my head to attach my wig.

"See you out there," he said, and went back down four flights of stairs.

What he didn't know was that I couldn't have run lines because I didn't remember any of my lines. Not one.

Backstage, both of us standing next to each other in the dark just before we were going to make our entrance, I realized I'd forgotten to get my props. I started to move to the table at the end of the stage to get them, and George grabbed my shoulder to stop me. I think he thought I was about to bolt the theater.

As the show opened, I had to carry George out onto the stage. Then his character asked me a question, to which I was supposed to give an answer that ended with the line: "They were coming and going at the same time."

I muffed it. I said, "going and coming at the same time." The audience sat mute.

George gave me a look. It lasted only a millisecond, but it said (even his look had that iconic raspy voice): **There is a line that appears once in**

**your life, a line you either walk over or step back from. This is that line . . . right here . . . right now. Your move!**

I got it. He pointed me through the scene—over there a table, over here a cup of water, over there a window—and the audience started laughing and I thought, **I'm gonna make it.**

In my peripheral vision, I could see the other actors coming to the curtains at the sides of the stage; they could see that I was getting it.

At the end of the performance, actors bow in billing order. I was the lowest face on the totem pole, so I went last. George stopped the audience from clapping and brought me stage-center. He said, "You don't understand, this is his first time."

I got quite an ovation.

Then he said, "You are going to hear things from this young man." It was generous and life-changing. Afterward, I went across the street to Sardi's. I walked in and they applauded. I had double helpings of the famous cannelloni.

I didn't sleep for two days; my adrenal glands were locked in the "on" position. When Héctor left the show, I was offered the role full-time. I would be paid $600 a week—a fortune. I thought I'd gone to heaven. I'd never made so much money in my life.

On the final day of negotiating, John Kimble, my then agent and a very nice man, called me and said, "I think we should turn it down."

Pause. Pause. Pause.

"Why in God's name would we turn this down? This is it!"

He said, "I can't get an 'and' in front of your name on the program or the poster outside."

Pause. Deep breath.

"Here's what we're going to do, John. You're going to call them back and say, 'My client accepts the role. And every night before he goes on, I will say under my breath, **and**.'"

Ever since, when someone brings up an "and" credit, I say, "I want two 'ands.'" They always think I'm kidding. In fact, here are all of the billings I'm still angling for:

**And . . . And Jeffrey Tambor**
**And Really . . . Jeffrey Tambor**
**And Wait Till You See This . . . Jeffrey
  Tambor**
**And Yep He's Still Acting . . . Jeffrey
  Tambor**
**And Perhaps for the Very Last Time . . .
  Jeffrey Tambor**

CUT TO: George's last week in the show, and the Shubert Organization threw him a party at Windows on the World, the late, great restaurant that used to perch atop the old World Trade Center. The entire cast and crew gathered for a splendid celebration. Canapés and liquor flowed as copiously as our love for George. He was a tough daddy to us, but we worshipped and respected him. George was in his cups and for some reason wearing a pith helmet with a sheer cloth covering his face. I was so grateful to him. Not only had he made my first night, it was thanks to him that I would take over Héctor's role full-time when he left.

I walked up to him. "George?"

"Yeah?"

"I just want to say thank you."

"Oh fuck you."

"Thank you."

"Ah fuck you."

"No really, thank you. What can I do for you?"

"Fuck off."

I walked away. I had just gotten a "George C. Scott."

Minutes later I was standing with another group of people in a different part of the restaurant when I felt a tap on my shoulder. I turned to find George.

"Help somebody," he said.

"What?"

"Help somebody," and he walked away.

Later, the notorious and powerful Bernie Jacobs and Gerald Schoenfeld walked into the room. Without missing a beat, George pulled the face cloth back down over his face and yelled, "Cover the food!"

• • •

I'd love to tell you my career was smooth sailing after George paved the way, but this was real life, not a Disney movie. When **Sly Fox** moved from Broadway to Los Angeles, Bob Dishy didn't join the cast, so I took his role as Abner Truckle. During rehearsals (which were always hellaciously early in the morning because George C. liked to tee off at the country club by noon), in the space beneath the stage at the Shubert Theatre, I was given the same blocking Bob Dishy had done in New York. I was literally re-creating his performance, and I was doing it very well. Arthur Penn was so proud. He would come into my dressing room and shake his head with a slight smile, and then he would give me notes.

On the last Friday morning before previews began the following Tuesday, Larry Gelbart came to watch our final run-through. And for the first time, I was off. All that "wait till you see the kid" talk had unnerved me. Eyes were on me, and I pressed too hard. I hit all the wrong beats. The looks on my cast mates' faces said, "What's wrong?" The more off I was, the more I pressed. I was in disasterland.

When we were done, Larry said just one sentence to me. I don't remember the exact words, but the gist was, "What's all the shootin' fer?"

It was like a death. I was married and had a very young daughter, but I was living in L.A. for the run, and my wife and daughter were back in New York. I had to go back to my empty house by myself, no one to talk to. I couldn't confess to my wife. I was too ashamed. I was alone from Friday through the weekend all the way up to Tuesday. I couldn't exercise. I had nothing to do but regret my lack of talent and worry that I was probably going to be fired. I tried to get ahold of Arthur Penn, anyone, but no dice. That I lived through that weekend is a miracle. I can still feel the ache in my solar plexus.

On Tuesday, I went to the theater. We did a light run-through before the evening's opening performance, and then I went to my dressing room to wait. Then there was a knock on the door. I opened the door, and standing there was Bea Arthur and her husband, and her friend Betty White and **her** husband, and the four of them crammed into my dressing room to wish me good luck.

Here's the thing: You never say hello to an actor before a show. It's bad luck. Thank God for the great John Heffernan, who came in and marshaled everybody out, saying, "This is not the way it's done. He needs to be alone."

Nonetheless, the performance went well. I said my first line—correctly—and it got a laugh. The laugh got me back, and I sailed through the show. Inside my brain, I said, **You're okay. You know what you're doing. You're going to make it.**

Afterward, Charles Nelson Reilly grabbed me and said, "Life is going to change." He took me to the after-party and we sat with the **L.A. Times** critic

Charles Champlin. I felt like visiting royalty from that moment on.

I never forgot that weekend in the desert. The emptiness, the self-doubt. I believe we all need to have that weekend in our lives. As George Eliot wrote, a man must have his thwackings.

## 9

*Gabriel   Eli   Kasia   Eve   Hugo   Molly*

# Lessons from Unexpected Masters

I am in awe of teachers. I've had many over the years, but several stand out for how much they inspired me—a handful actually saved my life. One of the key things I've learned in my career is how important it is to work with people who make you better. Sometimes we work with people out of obligation, but if they're not making us better, there's no point. Work with people who give you confidence, who have confidence in you.

This doesn't mean you'll always work with nice guys; far from it. In fact, I would be wary of nice guys. Forget about bedside manner. When I went all Sonja Henie in **Sly Fox,** Arthur Penn knocked me back to my senses and he wasn't nice about it. But even in that, he was giving me credit that I could handle it and correct my performance.

Many years after **Sly Fox,** I appeared in a Broadway revival of David Mamet's brilliant play **Glengarry Glen Ross,** directed by Joe Mantello. Joe is a great director, but he isn't huggy-kissy-feely-lovey. Every time he gave me a note, I got better. That's all I needed.

As we were nearing production, he came to my dressing room. **Knock knock knock.** He opened the door and said, "I can't hear you," and closed the door.

The next night, **knock knock knock.** "You've been doing too much film lately. Welcome back to the theater. Speak up."

The next night, **KNOCK KNOCK KNOCK.** "You need to speak up! I cannot hear you!"

And I got better. And Joe got a Tony. I will work with Joe Mantello anytime anywhere. Hi, Joe.

It is the same with acting teachers: work with teachers who make you better. There are too many

**poseurs** out there, too many people willing to take your money. There are only so many Harold Clurmans and Bobby Lewises in the world. Too often we get into the thrall of the mystique of the acting teacher, and we focus on pleasing the teacher. If you don't get better in the first two weeks of your acting class, for which you've plunked down a good amount of money, get the fuck out of there as fast as you can. Take it from one who didn't: I spent decades, actually two, **two** decades, pleasing an acting teacher. After a while, it gets counterproductive. You start to think the acting class is real and the outside world is unreal. The scene in the acting class is more important than your outside work.

Back in Shakespearean times, there was a system where a young actor would apprentice to an older actor. He would be the older actor's assistant, and he would watch the older actor and learn. Today I tell young actors, get on sets if you can and watch actors act. Go to the theater and watch actors act. Study them. Talk to them. Read books about acting. Get ahold of **Actors Talk About Acting** if you can, probably out of print.

But beware the pretenders, because that is dangerous territory. Remember, performing is performing your life. It's not comfortable, it's not safe, but it's real.

Teachers come in all shapes and sizes. These are some of mine.

## MY KIDS

**Childhood is the credit balance of the writer.**
—GRAHAM GREENE

My teachers now are my five children. My older daughter, Molly, is in her late thirties—she's forty-one—and a graduate of Smith College and Columbia University. Doctor Tambor now graces the campus of C. W. Post as Associate Professor of History, and as of this writing has published her first book, **The Lost Wave: Women and Democracy in Postwar Italy,** with Oxford University Press. (I'm a parent, what can I say—you never stop being proud.) Molly was born in Milwaukee when I was doing repertory theater there. My wife, Joyce, and I had gone to a Fourth of July concert in one of Milwaukee's famed parks, and Joyce said, "She's kicking to the John Philip Sousa." The next morning at 4:00 a.m., Molly was born at St. Mary's Hospital.

When Molly was an infant, my career was just starting to kick into high gear. I got my first Broadway role and my first film. Daddy's mind was unfortunately elsewhere engaged and my parenting skills were less than finely honed; regretfully, I gave Molly second billing while Papa worried and fretted about his career.

But I knew Molly was special. One day, after we'd moved to New York, I picked her up from her day care at a local synagogue on the Upper West Side of Manhattan. It was the Jewish festival of Purim and she was dressed up as Queen Esther. She had a golden tiara crowning her curly blond hair, and a long regal dress and a scepter. I will never forget the scepter; the scepter was key to the whole transformation of who she was—the star of the show. I was merely her attendant, as it should be.

As we walked down Broadway, cars honked at her and people on the sidewalk smiled and said hello. I think that was her red bowtie moment, when she realized that she was special. She was indeed Queen Esther, the Morning Star. By the time we got home, she was a different Molly—and the correct billing was reestablished in the Tambor household.

CUT TO: I am seventy-two years old, and I have an eleven-year-old son, Gabriel; a nine-year-old daughter, Evie; two six-year-olds, Hugo and Eli. I also have a grandson, Mason, who was born just a week after Gabriel. It doesn't make any sense. And it makes perfect sense. God, being the ironist that She is, gave me a second chance.

Here's what happened. My wife, Kasia, and I couldn't get pregnant. So we went to a fertility center in Los Angeles, where we were living at the time. **Arrested Development** had just been picked up for another season, which I actually found out from the finance officer at the center as we were passing by his office. Somehow, he got the news before I did and congratulated us as we walked down the corridor to our appointment. "Hey, great news on the pickup," he shouted as we headed toward yet another round of shots. Only in L.A. would the finance guy at a fertility clinic not only know the lingo, but know that my show was renewed before I did. Los Angeles, for good or ill, is that kind of town. We like New York. Everyone looks the same under the subway lighting; it's one of the great levelers.

Anyway, on the fertility front, nothing worked. It was heartbreaking. Many, many tears were shed. Many, perhaps too many, bottles of wine were consumed (Kasia) as well as many bottles of scotch (Jeffrey). Finally, we decided to adopt.

We met with an agency, and they found a wonderful young woman who was about to graduate from college. We met with her, and everything was arranged. A few months later, I was on set doing a scene with Jessica Walter when the call came: "Now. The baby is being born **now**." I had to drive to the

Valley to get to the hospital, but we had to finish the scene. Please understand, Jessica is one of our greats. When she finishes a scene, there is nothing left, not a crumb. She is an artistic killer. She is also a bit of a perfectionist, painstakingly exact with her craft. On that day, in that particular scene, Jessica kept restarting her lines to get it just right.

I kept saying, "Excuse me, a baby is being born."

She kept saying, "Oh, let me start again," and "Just one more." Until she finally got it.

I ran out into the parking lot, jumped in the car, and sped across town.

When Kasia and I got to the maternity ward at the hospital, our beloved Dr. Jay met us along with the head of the adoption agency. Jay said, "This is a **tough** baby."

I had never heard that phrase before and didn't quite know what it meant. We went into the NICU to see him.

All mothers know the following: infants have two survival instincts: one is sucking, so they can get milk; the other is grasping. As we stood over the bassinet, I put my index finger into the curve of that baby's tiny hand. As the adoption agency head said, "You don't have to accept this child," that baby was already grasping my finger. He was way ahead of us. And just like that, that child was **ours.** It was a life-changing moment.

Gabriel was born with something called VATER

syndrome, which is bad news. The syndrome affects the Vertebrae, Anus, Trachea, Esophagus, and kidneys (Renal). Medical science, for all its wisdom and learning, doesn't know why it happens. There's no blood test for this condition. It's not even a condition or disease per se, but a "nonrandom association of birth defects." In other words, you only know you have it if you have at least three symptoms on the menu of options. Gabriel had a full smorgasbord. He had to have a surgery before he was three months old to fix a tethered spinal cord.

I firmly believe that this was the universe's way of telling me, "Uh, excuse me? Mr. Tambor, sir? Mr. Big Important Actor, sir? Get off your lazy, self-involved ass, you're going to have to take care of somebody other than yourself."

Gabriel has had a tough time, but he turned out great. He knows he's a little different from other kids his age, he's a little smaller, and sometimes it bothers him. But one of the key things about VATER syndrome is that the brain is not affected by it. And indeed, Gabriel is extremely intelligent, reads constantly, and actually runs beautifully, if not as fast and gracefully as some of his peers. To this father, he is Nureyev.

"Teacher" doesn't even begin to describe Gabriel. This young child kicked our asses into service and changed every aspect of our lives.

Every six months, I take Gabriel to the great Dr. Michael Vitale at Columbia University Medical Center in New York for a checkup on his scoliosis, which is part of VATER syndrome. As part of the checkup, we go to the radiology department in the pediatric orthopedic wing for X-rays, and every time we go we get a lesson in how devastating this syndrome can be and how lucky Gabriel was to escape with as little trouble as he did. The thousand-yard gaze of the parents of these children is as sad a sight as I've ever seen.

In September 2016, we were invited to the White House for a tour. The guide kept asking arcane history questions and teeing himself up to provide the answer, but my Gabriel knew the answers to every question, including some obscure fact about the White House in 1814.

CUT TO: Father and Mother in the corner, patriotic hearts bursting with joy, or, as we say on my side of the street, kvelling.

He is so smart but is not always on the same plane as everyone else, certainly not Mom and Dad. In the stands at a recent Jets–Seahawks game, the crowd cheering at the top of their lungs, Gabriel turned to me and said, "The Jewish religion is really the foundation of Christianity." He thereby got the crown for king of the non sequitur. If there had been a camera on us, it would have shown a young boy smiling and an aging father staring straight ahead in stupefaction amid thousands of fans on all sides screaming, "JETS NATION!"

He is a fanatic about Carl Sagan and could watch Neil deGrasse Tyson on an endless loop. I recently caught him secretly downloading **Freakonomics** on his phone. His reading teacher has reported that he holds a book he brings from home beneath his desk during reading period, abjuring the teacher's selection of the day for something a little more to his taste and level. (Dad's own teacher sent a note home to Barney and Eileen about the very same thing.)

If you ask him a question, you'd better take a seat, because he loves to share and has no ability to read social cues that you are bored, or to realize that he has been talking for thirty minutes. I have actually left his room, gone downstairs to make coffee, and come back while he is still mid-lecture. Once, when I was doing a film with Michael Palin, the famous traveler and former Python, he asked Gabriel a question. Thirty minutes later, I looked over from where I was across the room and saw Michael signal to me with his eyes and neck to please come rescue him. That's my boy. "Kvell" doesn't even get near to how I feel about him.

More than anything, Gabriel is a beautiful soul. This angel, this teacher, came to Earth as a gift to Kasia and me. It's not always pleasant to realize how much more intelligent and better-looking he is than

I, but hey, those are the breaks. Remember: God is an ironist. Hi, Gabriel!

Around six o'clock on the morning of Gabriel's second birthday, we got the news that our second adopted child, Evie, was about to be born. We had planned a birthday party for later that day, so we called all the parents and had everyone come over right away for an early-morning party. Then we threw everybody out, jumped in the car, drove to the airport, and hopped on a plane to Albuquerque, New Mexico. We drove like possessed fiends to Mesa Hospital, where the birth was happening.

At the nursing station in the maternity ward, I said, "We're here for the Tambor baby?"

The woman looked at her computer. "Nope, no baby by that name here."

Turns out there are **two** Mesa hospitals in Albuquerque and we are at the wrong one. Oy. The possessed fiends turn to get back in the taxi to go to Mesa Hospital #2. There's no car. The driver has left. We are beside ourselves and scared out of our wits. We have to get to the hospital (the right one).

And then—oh, let's just call it a miracle, shall we?—a young nurse comes up to us as we are trying to reach our driver, the other hospital, the adoption agency, and offers to drive us. "Just wait for me by the elevator."

She leads us to her car, which is possibly the smallest car I've ever seen, perhaps one size up from the car that clowns spill out of at the circus. Kasia is in the front passenger seat and I'm crammed in the back, my knees crushed into my face as our savior drives us across this desert valley to the right hospital and we find our baby daughter, who has arrived safe and sound.

By the way, our savior-nurse's name? Angel. Can't make this shit up.

Three years later, God, continuing to share lessons in irony, sees to it that Mom and Dad Tambor get pregnant. (Drum roll.) With twins. Hugo and Eli, now age six—both came out peeing beautiful orange arcs of urine as they were airlifted from womb to bassinet.

So here's this award-winning actor's morning ritual. Ready?

Every morning, I get up, down the cold coffee that I left on the nightstand the evening before, and put out four thermoses of water with ice for backpacks. I do the vitamin cups for all four. I pour four milks—three low fat and one full fat for Gabriel. Two of the milks get heated. (Thank Polish grandmother for that one.) If it's summer, I put suntan lotion on all four, a hateful exercise that makes me slightly sick to my stomach because of the oleaginousness of it all. In winter, I make sure the boots are dry and ready for their trek in the snow to the bus stop. I might drive Gabriel to computer camp, the little ones to a talent show, and music lessons are on Friday. Evie has chorus at 8:15 in the morning, an acting class (please God no, not even funny), and

French lessons on Saturdays. Gabriel has a weekly appointment at 12:30 p.m. with Dr. Diane to discuss his week, and the twins have lacrosse at 5:00, which is the same time Evie has field hockey. (Did you know field hockey sticks are $150? Have you ever seen a field hockey stick? It's a stick.) There's a school get-together for kindergarten, and another for middle school. In the evening, I give Gabriel a shot of growth hormone in the **tuchus** and tell him to eat more. I have shot myself in my leg by mistake preparing this needle more than once, but have yet to grow an inch nor has any hair appeared on top of my head.

That is my glorious, glamorous life. Are you anybody? This is who I am. It's really tough, backbreaking, enormously frustrating—and I love it. They have reminded me of the power of parenthood, the enthusiasm of childhood. It's made me a better actor and a better person. Having this family cuts the time off everything. I don't have time for the neurotic horseshit I used to do. Get to the theater three hours ahead of time? No time. Learning my lines and everyone else's? No time. Worry about whether they like me? **Is that the right take?** No time. No time. No time.

I've also been blessed with a second chance through my children. As I write this, Gabriel is beginning his first year of middle school. His mother and I took him to an orientation about a week before opening day where the students and parents met the teachers, and the kids were assigned lockers. It's a rite of passage that dates back decades if not centuries, when kids move from cubbies up to lockers.

When the time came, Gabriel stood in front of his locker with the combination in his hand. I stood a few paces behind him to let him do his thing. Try as he might, he couldn't open the locker. The more he tried, the more rattled he got. He burst into tears, and so did I.

See, sixty years ago, when faced with my first locker, I couldn't get it open. I tried again. Couldn't do it. After the third time, I gave up. I found a curtained-off nook outside Mr. World's geometry classroom, and that's where I kept my books **for four years.**

That was not going to be Gabriel's fate. We snuck into the school over Labor Day weekend. There were a few staff members around and one asked us what we were doing.

"We're just going to check out my son's locker," I said.

"Let me help you. I'll bring a key."

"No, no, thank you. We can do this."

We walked off toward Gabriel's locker. "I think I need to stop off at the bathroom," he said, but then just kept walking to his locker.

He stood in front of that lock. He'd been up all night thinking about it. He began: Right to 7. Left to 37. Right to 27. I stood back and watched him. He failed once. He failed twice. **God, two days in**

**a row, he can't open his locker.** He failed a third time.

I stepped over and said, "I think you have to go all the way around once, and then stop at the number, and then go all the way around the other direction and go to the next number."

I stood back. **Pull it up. Pull it up. Pull it up.**

And then **click.** Gabriel opened his locker. The look on his face when he turned around—it was as if I'd won twenty Emmys, eight Golden Globes, five SAG Awards, and a standing ovation. He grabbed my hand and started to walk away.

"I thought you needed to use the bathroom," I said, trying not to let him see the tears in my eyes.

"I brought my chamois so I could clean my glasses to see the numbers better, but I didn't need to."

My reward for all of this is arguing with people at my local Dunkin' Donuts when I bring my children along for my morning coffee run.

"Are these your grandchildren?"

"No, they're my children.

"No, they're not. They're your grandkids."

"They're my kids."

"No way."

"Way."

"Kids, is this your father?"

If you have the least bit of doubt, why would you ask, "Are these your grandkids?" And then why would you **argue about it**?

Then, every night, Gabriel says, "Good night,

Dad. I love you. See you in the morning." (He says, "See you in the morning" in his good-night texts when I am away filming, even though he won't see me in the morning.) This patter outdoes Robert Frost—it kills me. It makes my heart, and just about everything else, ache. For a long time, I thought my tombstone would say AND JEFFREY TAMBOR, but now I'm thinking SEE YOU IN THE MORNING is an option. Stay tuned.

Gabriel taught me to be outside myself. And he taught me humor. That kid makes me laugh more than anyone.

Evie is feminine and expressive and takes shit from no one. As I was driving her home from oh-myGodIdon'tknowwhatI'lldoifshegoesthrough-withthis acting class, she said, "What is it you do again?" She can't figure out what the hell I do when I'm at home. When I'm writing, I like to keep the TV on in the background. She thinks I watch television all day, that that's my job. I'm terrified that's what she tells her friends and teachers at school.

Eli is fairly serious and has mastered Joe Cool. Where he got that, no one knows. There is certainly no model for that in our house. He has taught me focus. He's all about being a big boy. I see **hedge fund** in the future. He's the kid who goes to the top of the big kids' slide and just as you're about to say, "I don't know, Eli, maybe you shouldn't—" he's **whoosh,** down to the bottom. He's taught me a lot about courage.

I once told Hugo that I was going to give a lecture to a group of teachers, and I told him I was a bit nervous about it. I asked him if there was anything I should tell the teachers. He said, "Tell them you need to buy some hair." He's reading a elephant-and-piglet book about the importance of saying "thank you." There's no more to be said.

I could write a whole book on what my children teach me every day, but until then, here's the **Reader's Digest** version:

**Be an Amateur—a Lover**
**Be Audacious**
**Be Outlandish**
**Be Fearless**
**Be Reckless**
**Be Passionate**
**Be Ugly**
**Be Dangerous**
**Be Illogical**
**Be Tasteless**
**Be Careless**
**Be Loud (as in live out loud)**
**Be Incorrect**
**Be Wild**
**Be an Artist**
**Be Emotional**
**Be a Bad Boy/Bad Girl**
**Be Silly**
**Be Big-Big-Hearted**

**Be Impulsive**
**Be Intuitive**

Fuck 'em. (Thank you, Sir Richard Burton.)
Thank you, Tambor family. You're the greatest award of all. See you in the morning.

### "ATTABOY"

When I was doing **Arrested Development,** I never watched the show much because I didn't like to watch myself on screen. It used to make Jason Bateman crazy angry. He'd ask me what I thought of an episode, and I'd confess I hadn't seen it. "You know, a few of us around here could use an 'attaboy' once in a while." **Bing!** A light went off. He was totally right.

I have learned a lot of things in my seven-plus decades. One is that looking forward to senior discounts is stupid, because by the time you get discounted movie tickets, it's still orders of magnitude more expensive than when you were a kid. Ticket price in 1955: 25 cents; in 2016 with senior discount: $9.

I can't do anything about the price of movie tickets—that part of the business is "above my pay grade," as they say. But I have learned two lifesaving secrets that have indeed saved my life, even though I forget them pretty much every other day and have to be reminded of them by my wife and kids.

The first one is, admittedly, going to make a lot of people roll their eyes: **Adore everything.** (Go ahead, roll away.) I was taught this tenet by the great acting teacher Milton Katselas, and it was taught to **him** by the great writer James Leo Herlihy. When people ask me for one salient piece of life advice and I tell them, "Adore everything," they are usually disappointed. But it's a true thing, and you should do it.

The second secret is: **"Attaboy."** It's not "There's a boy," or "Thatta boy"—any schmuck can say, "Thatta boy." Grammatical correctness is not the point. This is straight-from-the-gut passion. This is about setting someone up for learning and success. This is praise, motherfucker, and as far as I'm concerned, it's the secret of life. It's how you get to adore everything. It comes from your heart, and it's essential in teaching and in art and pretty much in everything else.

When my son Gabriel was nine years old, he joined a lacrosse team. He's not as fast as other kids his age, so my wife and I were so nervous for him before the first practice. Let me be clear: Gabriel is not the best lacrosse player I have ever seen. Gabriel is a good fencer, a genius strategist, reads constantly, and has a mind of incomprehensible nuance and beauty, but he's a bit lost on the lacrosse field. It's not his fault, he just is. (Trust me, you wouldn't want to see me out there either.)

When we got to the field, I went up to the coach and told him about Gabriel's situation. "He's so invested here, he so wants to make a connection. And we're so worried for him."

The coach said, "I hear you. I'm glad you talked to me. Don't worry, I got it."

The kids went off to their practice, and I sat on the sidelines working on my script and I hear the coach yell, "Attaboy, Gabriel! Attaboy!"

I looked up, and there was my son running midfield. He was having the time of his life. He wasn't ready to go pro or anything like that, but it was beautiful. He was so happy and energized and delighted to be out there. With every "attaboy," I could see his confidence grow. To be honest, I didn't think he'd have the stamina to make it through the first hour of practice, but he sailed through two hours. And then three hours. During water breaks, he'd come up and burble and gurgle his joy at me (I couldn't understand a word he said because he had a mouth guard smooshed up in his mouth). At the end of practice, I heard his friends say to him, "Gabriel, I've never seen you run like that."

That coach was a true teacher. And "attaboy" was his secret weapon.

The next morning, Gabriel got up happier and sunnier than I'd seen him in a long time. When he sat down for his daily fifteen minutes of piano—and he is not Arthur Rubinstein either—he played 50 percent better than he'd ever played before. "Attaboy" floats all boats.

The first time I experienced this myself was at Aptos Junior High School when I wasn't much older than Gabriel was at his first lacrosse outing. I was a mess—I was husky, I had a lisp, and because I'd skipped a grade, I didn't understand a thing. One of my teachers called my parents to complain that I was singing in the back of the class.

My mother said, "Okay, thank you. We'll have a talk with him. By the way, what's he singing?"

The teacher said, "Something about 'I don't understand anything.'"

I received a report card that was all F's and an Unsatisfactory (in Citizenship); that's how unhappy I was. All I cared about was lunch. I would run to the cafeteria and have two scoops of mashed potatoes with gravy and French fries. The woman in the hairnet who served me would say, "Please, you have to stop doing this to yourself."

But, first period, I had drama class with Jim Pravettoni, or Mr. Prav, as we called him. He had wavy Italian hair and wore a nice suit and glasses, a little bit like my idol Steve Allen. He was the coolest;

he let us drink coffee in the teachers' lounge when we rehearsed on weekends. And his class was magic. We did a play called **Elmer Across the Footlights,** which we rehearsed after school. I learned the lines but they didn't make much sense to me. One day, I was rehearsing with a girl named Emma who was a bit of a goody-two-shoes. All of a sudden I decided to improvise. The other kids in the play stopped, and I just ran with it.

Emma walked off the stage, saying, "Mr. Prav, Jeffrey's not doing it right."

From the audience, Mr. Prav said, "Leave him alone. He knows what he's doing."

**I know what I'm doing?** No one had ever told me I knew what I was doing. In fact, I had it on pretty good authority that I did **not** know what I was doing—at home, especially at home.

In the Kabuki theater tradition of Japan, when an actor does especially well on a turn or a pose or a moment, you will hear people in the audience shout something that sounds to my Western ear like "Hoo-dee-yah!"

I asked someone what the shouting meant, and he said, "There you are."

Years ago when I was in Tokyo attending the Kabuki-za theater, a young actor came out to stage-center. He was probably five or six years old. He faced the audience and robotically said his line. I could see actors crowding the wings on both sides of the stage to listen to this first-time thespian. When he finished the place went wild, from the sides of the stage to the top balconies. This child actor was being "attaboyed" into the theater.

It's what Mr. Prav said: "He knows what he's doing."

**I know what I'm doing. I actually know what I'm doing.**

Years ago, I was doing a film with a first-time director I'd never met before. When it was time to do my first scene, the director said, "I'm going to give you a direction. Would you mind . . . ?" and he handed me one of those Chia heads—you know, the bald head you smear seeds on and it grows "hair"? That's what he thought my character should be holding in his hand for this scene. It was singularly the worst, most obtuse piece of direction I have ever received.

The crew was all there standing by, arms crossed, watching. It's the first day of shooting and there are millions and millions of dollars at stake. And this director is going with the Chia head. The crew was waiting to see my reaction.

I looked at him for a moment, took a breath, and said, "Okay." I took the head and we did the scene, but I made sure to hold that head out of the frame, down around my midsection, and I signaled the cameraman so he understood.

When we finished the scene, the director came over to me to apologize. I think he realized he wasn't at his best. I noticed that his hands were shaking.

He was scared out of his wits, so I told him that it took great guts to give that direction.

Every day, I just kept acknowledging him, and you know what? He started to really direct me, and he got better and better and better. He was a good director, but like all of us he was exhausted from bench-pressing fear all day. The crew had gone from cynical to supportive. By the end of the shoot, we were both knocking it out of the park.

He just needed an "attaboy," just like Gabriel. Just like me. I'm the guy who wants an "attaboy" when I take out the garbage.

You'll often find me at my local Dunkin' Donuts in the morning after my kids have gone to school. There is a counterperson there I see from time to time. She also works at the local grocery, and sometimes I see her having a cigarette break before she starts her shift at the donut shop. The other day, I stopped to say hello during her smoke before I went inside.

"So you work a shift at the grocery and come straight here to do another shift?"

She said yes. I asked if she had family and told her how impressed I was that she could put in that kind of day. "You are such an inspiration," I said. "I'm going to tell my children about this."

Her face changed and her eyes shone bright. I think she was near tears—I mean, she was exhausted. I don't think anybody had ever asked how she was.

Later, inside the shop, when I got my coffee, I looked down and there were half a dozen bagels. The next morning at breakfast, I told my kids where the bagels came from and why. Someone said "Attagirl."

You don't have to be visibly struggling to appreciate an "attaboy." When I was filming **Meet Joe Black** in Providence, I called Marty Brest, the director, late one night. "Hi, this is Jeffrey. I just wanted to say you're doing a great job." There was silence. "Did I say something wrong?" He said no one had ever told him that. Marty was a pro and had a slew of successful films like **Beverly Hills Cop** and **Scent of a Woman** under his belt, but I knew, when even very accomplished people close the door at night, they shake just like the rest of us.

You have to work with people who give you praise, who give you confidence. Avoid those who don't. They are to be put on a shelf and taken down only for Thanksgiving and Hanukkah.

On the **Transparent** set, our creator Jill Soloway has "attaboy" in her DNA. There is praise all over that set. Jill starts and ends the day with it. It's behind the camera, in front of the camera, up in the production offices, in editing, in the costume and makeup trailers, in transportation. It's in the food, I tell you. Praise is the heart and soul of Jill and that show.

Legendary actor and director Orson Welles described a time he was filming the movie **Touch of Evil** and felt that he was flailing as both actor and director. When the camera was on him, he kept flubbing his lines. His costar, Akim Tamiroff, was in the scene with him but just off camera. When Orson yelled "Cut!" on his own scene, Mr. Tamiroff came over to him and whispered in his ear, "You're the man." That's all it took. Orson Welles said he never looked back from that moment. The praise clinched it.

This is how Orson Welles put it: "You have to make the actor believe he is better than he is. That is the job. More than confidence, give him arrogance. He really has to think he's great, that he is extraordinary."

"Arrogance" literally means **to take up space.** In other words, there you are.

## SUPPORT

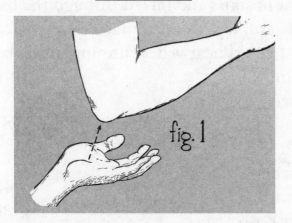

fig. 1

His name was David, and he came into Mrs. Painter's third-grade class at Westlake Elementary School in the middle of the school year. He wore glasses, his head was big and shaped sort of like a peanut, verging on that classic extraterrestrial look, and he sported a constant and unwavering smile. He was doomed from the moment he walked in. He was immediately shunned.

I was on my own most mornings before school. My father drove Larry to school, and my mom was firmly ensconced in the bathroom with her first vodka and lime juice of the day. I would pour myself cornflakes and milk, and then get dressed for school: shirt, pants, shoes.

One morning, I couldn't find my belt. I checked the closet: no belt. The floor: nothing. Under the bed: just some empty Hostess Twinkie wrappers and the headgear/face chastity belt that I was supposed to wear at night attached to my braces but never did. There was no belt anywhere.

I went upstairs and talked through the bathroom door, the full-length mirror facing me so I could see myself. I could hear water running in the bathtub.

"Mom!"

Silence.

"Mom! Ican'tfindmybeltdoyouknowwhereitis-Mom?"

Silence.

"Mom?"

Toilet flush.

"Okay, Mom. See you after school."

I searched frantically. My pants wouldn't stay up without a belt. And then I remembered the toy gun and holster set I was given for Hanukkah several years earlier. I opened the toy chest, took out the belt, removed the faux silver Hopalong Cassidy gun, and put the belt on. Pants secured, I—gulp—left for school.

When I walked into the play yard, there was no subtle transition or dawning realization. It didn't begin with a murmur or a handful of giggles. No, the kids burst into full-throated laughter as they pointed at my waist. When the class bell rang and we went inside, the laughter turned into snorting and snickering, which seemed to bite even more. I'm pretty sure Mrs. Painter joined in when I went up to the pencil sharpener during class.

It seemed like forty years elapsed before the recess bell rang. And then, **brrrrrrrnnnggg!**—salvation was at hand.

I made sure to hang back so that I was at the tail end of the line of students exiting the building. Smiling David fell in step with me as I headed for the chain-link fence that ran along the outer perimeter of the playground. I sat down on a bench. David sat with me. He didn't say a word. He didn't offer solace or comfort, no "there, there," or "life is hard," or "I'm with you, big guy." He just sat there, smiling that smile of his that was probably the custom among his people from outer space.

The bell rang at the end of recess, and my silent partner and I walked back to class. And I was So. Much. Better. The snickering seemed to die down, and I didn't care anyway. I made it through the day, because David, my first buddy, didn't care what kind of belt I wore or that it had a cowboy holster. He was just there when I needed someone to be there. Hi, David. Thanks.

CUT TO: When I give my lecture/talk/one-man show—I never know what to call it—I ask the audience members to put one hand underneath the elbow of the opposite arm. As they do so, I let them absorb the sensation. "That, ladies and gentlemen, is what support feels like."

When I was in my first film, **And Justice for All,** I was nervous. I didn't know what a "mark" was. I didn't know what an "apple box" was; I thought it was a box for apples—rather than something you put your props on—and when they asked me if I wanted one I said: "No thanks, I'll wait for lunch." I didn't know what a dressing room was. I didn't know what "crafty" was; it was craft service; I didn't know what craft service was. I didn't know what "cut" meant. I didn't know what a close-up was. I didn't know what a medium shot was. I didn't know what a master shot was. When someone handed me the call sheet, I memorized it because I didn't know what else to do with it. I thought the treats on the craft service table were for the producers.

The brilliant Norman Jewison must have clocked my fear. We were about to do the pivotal bathroom scene, and Norman led me to the set with his hand cupping my elbow as he guided me. It was the lightest of touches, but it was all I needed.

And that right there has always been my image of
a teacher: someone putting their hand under your
elbow and supporting you, guiding you. That's what
you want to seek in your life: that perfect hand that
says, **I got you.**

When people ask me what's my favorite film,
without hesitation I cite **Being There** with Peter
Sellers. That is what this whole David thing was
and is all about—just being there. It's what I didn't
have with my parents, and what I have to slap myself
daily to remember—**be there be there be there**—
with and for my kids. It has been a beast for me to
learn. I am prone to endless bouts of feeling sorry
for myself and storming out of restaurants. Kasia
has to remind me of our responsibility to the kids
when I start muttering, "I'm too old for this, I only
have a few years left!" (I'm nothing if not dramatic.)

But from the time the four of them step off their
several buses at the end of the school day, their mom
and I are there to serve, to be there, to be present and
connect. Tell my Evie that she's great, and she will
come through just fine, even though she doesn't
understand one word on her vocabulary homework,
or that "epidemic" is not being used correctly when
you say, "Gus [our dog] is an epidemic." Tell Hugo,
"It's okay to make mistakes" when he tries to read
and struggles to overcome his embarrassment at not
knowing how to do it perfectly. Yes, Eli, I will take
your hand and go with you upstairs to the bathroom
because you had a bad dream last night and are

wary of rooms with shadows. Gabriel, my love, we will make it through. You are my hero, my survivor, the kid who has overcome so many hurdles. You are safe, and I am there for you, a lesson I learned from David on the playground all those years ago.

Thanks for the support, David. Thanks for coming to Earth.

## <u>THE POWER OF STORY, OR LIES, LIES, LIES</u>

There were three rituals in Mrs. Painter's third-grade class.

### RITUAL #1

Once a month, always on a Wednesday, a speech teacher from outside the school came to test us. She was older and brittle—think Maggie Smith in **Downton Abbey** and take away the humor, flair, and fashion sense. She would stand at the front of the room, and as she called our names, we were to stand by our desk and count to ten. She would work her way up and down the rows until she got to me in the last row. If you had a defect in your speech, you had to leave the class and go to a different classroom to do exercises with her.

"Jeffrey?"

I stood up.

"Begin, please."

"One. Two. Three. Four. Five. Shikss."

"Out!"

Every month, I endured this humiliation.

## RITUAL #2

Every Monday, certain members of our class were dismissed early. These were the Catholic kids, and they went to the gym for the catechism class. My grandfather would refer to this fortunate group as the "goyim." Apparently we had a lot of goyim in our class, because on Monday afternoon, it was just John, Eddie, and me. We few Jews in a room.

## RITUAL #3

On Wednesdays, the girls who were Brownies were allowed to wear their uniforms to school because they had their weekly meeting Wednesday afternoons. One of those Brownies was Susan Pfotenhauer (don't hurt yourself, the **p** is silent). She had an angelic countenance that gave new meaning to the word **shiksa.** Susan was my first love. She didn't know I was alive. I gazed at her back from the seat in the rear of the classroom. When she got up to use the pencil sharpener, I got up too so I could stand near her.

So here's the ritual: it was called "story." Every morning, Mrs. Painter asked the class if anyone had something they wanted to share with the class. This involved standing in the front of the room, and nobody wanted to do it except Ted, who would announce who he was going to beat up after school.

One Wednesday, when Susan was in her fetching brown uniform, I raised my hand for "story." I walked up to the front and realized that this was my chance. I started talking about a fictitious fight my parents had the previous night. I played both parts, and I threw in a few Yiddish words and threats of physical violence to spice it up. I had Susan's undivided attention. I existed. She smiled. Susan Pfotenhauer smiled at the little Jewish villager who had come forth from his hut to tell his story.

I was captivated by the power of the story. Forget the truth, these lies were powerful and affecting. **If they can make Susan smile, they can do anything.**

That night, Mrs. Painter called my parents. The phone conversation was long. I believe my performance was recounted in full. My parents had to convince Mrs. Painter that everything was okay and everybody was safe, it was just that their son had a flair for the dramatic.

Some years ago, I told this story on a late-night talk show and even gave a shout-out to my long-ago first love: "Hi, Susan!"

A few weeks later I received a letter from her son, who had seen the show and recognized that it must have been his mother I was talking about. He called to tell her about it, and my Susan's reply was: "I don't know him." He felt it was his duty to let me know. Hi, Susan.

## <u>THANK YOU, ERNEST BORGNINE</u>

Saturdays were my day when I was a kid. On Saturday, I would go to the children's matinee at the Serra Theater in Daly City. I made the trek, which took nearly an hour across the valley and up the hill, on my own. My dad would give me a dollar, which could buy:

| Hot dog | 25 cents |
| Popcorn | 15 cents |
| Soda | 10 cents |
| Three Musketeers | 10 cents |
| Another soda | 10 cents |
| Another Three Musketeers | 10 cents |
| Another soda | 10 cents |

And I still went home with a dime in my pocket.

Note: I recently took my three little ones to the matinee in nearby Connecticut, a forty-minute drive. There have been some changes since I went to the Serra. A child's ticket is $9. That's $27 for the three. Add another senior ticket for $9—fuck you, it's not our fault you're old. If you buy them ahead of time online so you don't have to wait in line, that's another $1 per ticket. That's $40 before we've even gotten in the car.

I get to the ticket booth to pick up the tickets, and the clerk says, "I enjoy your work." Then asks for ID. (I'll pause while that sinks in.)

At the concession counter, which isn't a counter, it's an entire marketplace of carbohydrates and corn syrup, I order three popcorns and one large water.

"May I have an extra bag, so I can split up the three popcorns among the four of us?" I ask.

"We can't do that, sir."

"How come?"

"Corporate does a bag count. The money has to even up. By the way, I enjoy your work."

"Thank you. If I take a selfie with you, will you give me an extra bag?"

"Yes, sir!" And then, "That'll be $29.60."

Twenty-nine dollars and sixty cents is a pair of shoes, or a belt at least. It's half a massage.

We go inside the theater and take our seats. In my day, a kid's movie started with a cartoon or three. Road Runner and—the best of the best—Tom and Jerry. I couldn't get enough. Now, no cartoon. Instead, there are 740 coming attractions at a noise level like a flight deck on an aircraft carrier. The A/C is on so high, I develop an ice-cream headache just from breathing.

When I was little, the kids' feature usually finished by four o'clock, before the grown-up films (not "adult," that's a whole other deal) were shown. One careless afternoon when I was ten years old, I decided to stay. I sat in the darkened theater, the first of many days I would spend in darkened theaters, and waited while the staff came in with brooms and wastebaskets to clean up.

At 5:00 p.m., the evening rotation of films began with just me and a few other people in attendance for the early showing. First a cartoon—the adults got one too—and then the first feature: **Marty,** written by the great Paddy Chayefsky. The film was about a hapless working stiff who still lived with his mom in the Bronx. They were an Italian American family, and it was the mother's mission to get Marty the butcher married off to a nice girl. There was one problem:

Marty wasn't played by Cary Grant or Errol Flynn or Rock Hudson; he was played by Ernest Borgnine. Ernest Borgnine was not movie-star handsome. He was plain, ordinary, fat. His character is resigned to his fate as a bachelor until he meets the "plain" Clara, played by Betsy Blair.

This movie would change how Hollywood cast films forever after. It also changed me. Here was a guy who looked like me. Even though I was a kid, I related to this guy on the screen.

"Mama, I'm a dime a dozen," Marty said, and I cried. It was the first time I realized someone like me—ordinary, overweight, with a lisp—could maybe get the girl. But it was more than that. I already knew I wanted to be an actor, and seeing a guy like that starring in this movie gave me confidence in my dream. I walked home that night in the dark to explain to my parents why I was late. But I held on to that secret: **If Ernest can do it, so can I.**

The following Saturday, I brought two dollars and I stayed again. This week the film was **The Seven Year Itch** with Marilyn Monroe and Tom Ewell. Ewell played businessman Richard Sherman, whose family leaves Manhattan for summer vacation in Maine while he stays behind in the hot and humid city. He meets the knockout blonde who moves in upstairs and he's smitten. Ewell had played the role on Broadway, and some daring entrepreneur had the courage to put this ordinary-looking guy on the screen opposite Marilyn fucking Monroe, the bombshell of the nation and my generation. His performance was flawless—light, satirical, and underplayed beautifully. With every move he made, he seemed to give me implicit orders: **Go, there's a place for you.**

Thank you, Ernie.

Thank you, Mr. Ewell.

Thank you, Serra Theater.

I wouldn't be here without you.

## <u>MY DATE WITH SUSAN LEVY</u>

As a teenager, I had two lives. There was the theater life, and there was this Jewish life. The theater life was real; the Jewish life was faux. It was a role I played. Part of that role was dating nice Jewish girls. It was an unspoken rule in the Tambor house that the Tambor boys would not date shiksas. I didn't care about dating; I wanted to be an actor. I was monomaniacal about acting.

Nonetheless, I belonged to a Jewish fraternity called Aleph Zadik Aleph, or AZA. It was the boys' group of the B'nai B'rith Youth Organization, and the girls' group was cleverly called B'nai B'rith Girls, or BBG. AZA had a meeting every Wednesday night in the Richmond District. I was the editor of the newsletter, which I wrote late and at the last minute on Tuesday night and mimeographed. (Yes, I said "mimeographed.") We had conventions, and there were parties.

My first attempt at dating was going to a supper event of AZA and BBG with Susan Levy. She had short, curly hair and braces, and she wasn't particularly nice. Keep in mind, I was no treasure myself. I was overweight (husky), I had a lisp and braces, and I had my flannel pajamas under my wool slacks, just like I did at my bar mitzvah. I wasn't old enough to drive, so her parents had to take us to the venue. Oh, and I had a cold.

At this time in my adolescence, I was really starting to resent being Jewish. I resented being other. I resented looking different. I resented this supper where all the kids seemed to know each other and I didn't know anyone. I didn't know how to eat a meal with other people. In our house, dinner was twenty minutes and done and often on TV trays. Don't even get me started on which fork was for what. I had no in here. I wasn't witty. People couldn't understand what the fuck I was saying because of the lisp. And I didn't look right from the waist down.

We were having our first course, the salad, when someone said something funny and people laughed. In the silence that followed, I sneezed so forcefully that I farted. Nobody spoke. Nobody laughed. The look on Susan Levy's face changed from mild disinterest to hatred. We hadn't even had our entrée yet. We were still at salad.

In that mortification, one thing solidified for me. I was going to have to be a character actor, because there was no way I was going to be a romantic leading man. Ever. And I don't care if you don't remember me—hi, Susan!

## <u>THE GUY IN THE BOOKSTORE</u>

Lots of people read before bed; I **start** every single day reading. This is my ritual (and it almost ended my marriage): I make a cup of coffee before bed and put it on my nightstand. This routine goes all the way back to my college days. When I wake, I drink the cold coffee and read for thirty minutes. I don't get out of bed until I've completed this sacred ritual. (I'm on my twelfth Kindle.) For me, reading isn't just what I read—whether it's a novel, nonfiction, my beloved **New Yorker**—it's the actual act itself. The reading is the core of the question "Are you anybody?" I've been in synagogues, churches, mosques, the "rooms" where the higher-power thing is talked about, and I always come up short. I nod along with the crowd so I won't appear the apostate, but to me reading is submitting to another—and yes, a "higher"—power. It is submitting to a physical and mental yearning that is above and beyond and more.

Confession: I'm not sure the following is the truth. When I look back on it, it seems ethereal, like a dream.

When I was at Wayne State University in Detroit, there was this old musty bookstore on Woodward Avenue, which was owned by a Greek gentleman with a permanent two-day growth of beard and a palpable sneer as I walked the aisles of his store. The bookstore was a shambles and it had that musty old-book smell that I am addicted to. I loved to look through all the books. The owner would watch me. Well, he would always check where I was in the store, but he wouldn't look at me. I'd pick out a book, maybe sit down and read a little bit. Then I'd walk around some more. I loved this place. It felt like a sanctuary in the middle of the inner city.

I would go day after day—before rehearsal, after rehearsal—walk the aisles or sit in the rickety chair at the back of the store next to the bathroom with the OUT OF ORDER sign and meet some new friends: Philip Roth; Doris Lessing; Flannery O'Connor; Joseph Heller and his devastating parody of war in **Catch-22;** Kurt Vonnegut; J. D. Salinger; D. H. Lawrence; Shirley Hazzard; Joyce Carol Oates; Bernard Malamud. Saul Bellow took my breath away with **Mr. Sammler's Planet.** I was captivated by Thomas Mann's **Death in Venice.**

As Mr. Scowl and I got used to each other, our relationship started to change. He would mutter, "What play are you doing now?" and I would answer, **"Becket"** or **"Twelfth Night"** or **"Major Barbara."** When it came time to leave, there would be an old battered copy of George Bernard Shaw's letters next to the cash register. Mr. Scowl wouldn't say anything, but I would covertly obey and buy it. I would spend the next weeks devouring Shaw on just about every subject from Fabianism to Socialism in my little apartment. Later it would be George Meredith, Isaac Bashevis Singer, Fitzgerald, Hemingway.

Mr. Scowl became my teacher. One day he left a copy of **A Moveable Feast** at the register. He just nodded down to it, didn't say anything. The copy was thin and falling apart. He didn't ring it up—it was a gift. It is still my most treasured book, and I have underlined so many passages, it is starting to look like one of my scripts.

Every visit, he introduced another subject, another book recommendation. We would have discussions about what I'd read. We'd talk so long, the store would close, and I'd still be there talking. He would get a shot glass and pour a mysterious milky liquid into it (ouzo?) and hold forth. He didn't offer me anything. He still never made eye contact with me, which gave the conversations a feeling of the confessional, and he was the priest. He had no sense of humor, which fed my sense of something holy taking place. And indeed, he turned me into a reader, into a lover of books.

The power and draw of reading continues in the next generation. When my daughter Molly's kindergarten teacher asked her mother and me to come in for a conference, I went to the actor's go-to: drama. **"Mr. Tambor, your daughter . . . is learning-deficient. Cannot play with others. Is throwing lit matches at the other kids. Wants to be called Gwendolyn. Is speaking in tongues."** In real life (IRL, as the Internet says), the teacher said, "Your daughter is gifted. You have a responsibility to nurture it." The first big clue came when Molly had gone AWOL one day and no one could find her—until they discovered her in the cloakroom reading.

Every evening around five thirty, I begin the reading-with-kids ritual I call "Jeffrey Tambor on Tour of the Second Floor of Our House." First, I visit the little ones, Hugo and Eli. I've read **Good-**

**night Moon** so many times, I can recite it from memory. Same with Dr. Seuss. Eli likes to read fast and show his expertise to his brother. Hugo is having a little trouble with "th" and "ch" and he's afraid to make mistakes, but he reads to Eli and me, and walks around the house holding his prized Elephant and Piggie **The Thank You Book,** which I believe he has memorized.

Around 6:00 p.m. I head to Evie's room, where I find her lying on her bed in her pajamas, her hair wrapped in a towel from her shower. When we still lived in L.A., before the twins were born, I was reading to Evie one night, the two of us lying side-by-side on her bed with her magic reading lamp—all you have to do is gently touch it with your hand and it goes on. I was about mid-book, a reliable Dr. Seuss, and then, unprompted, Evie began to haltingly read with me. She was **reading.** I was there when the red light turned to green, the synapses fired, and her life began. Now Evie reads to me with perfect enunciation, never missing a beat. It is pure bliss. Right now she's humming along with Judy Blume. Judy Blume has enhanced the lives of all the Tambor children, and deserves the words "National Treasure" under her picture. Thank you, Judy.

By six thirty I'm in Gabriel's room. "Give me your **tuchus,**" I say, which is code for **I am going to give you your shot.** He gets 1.5 mcgs of growth hormone each night, and it's working. He's getting taller, and at eleven has more pubic hair than I have ever had. He is always reading when I "shoot him up." As I type this, Gabriel is reading Ron Chernow's **Alexander Hamilton.** It's the biggest book I've ever seen. He just finished Orwell's **1984,** which I read in my youth as a book about the future, and he's reading as history. (I'll pause to let this sink in.)

And now I am the proud co-owner of a bookstore in Los Angeles. (I live in New York—welcome to the spot-on entrepreneurship of the Tambors.) It's called Skylight Books, at 1818 North Vermont Avenue, and up until October 2016 it was managed by the genius Kerry Slattery, who also studied with Jack Cook at San Francisco State College. I'm hardly there, but I have introduced authors there. The calendar is filled with author events, writers debuting their work—Dave Eggers, Jonathan Safran Foer, my beloved **Transparent** teachers Zackary Drucker and Rhys Ernst, Megan Abbott, the list goes on and on and on.

I love to walk the aisles and see people with books open. It kills me. And the staff are dedicated readers themselves; they actually know and have read the books.

And—wait for it—we run a profit. It's not enough to buy Teslas for everyone on staff, but a profit. Skylight Books. Check it out. You can order online at skylightbooks.com! Tell them Beppy sent you.

All this from that guy in the bookstore in Detroit who drank ouzo and gently led me to "other places, other rooms." Thank you. I don't even know your name.

## BEFORE THERE WAS JILL, THERE WAS JILL

As the twentieth century came to a close, my life was in, shall we say, transition. **Larry Sanders** had ended, as had my marriage to Katie. A sitcom that I had been cast in, written by the great Mitch Hurwitz, sputtered after only four episodes. I was living alone and drinking so much that I had developed gout. Who gets gout? Henry VIII had gout. And now the Mayor of Whoville had gout. Yes, to top off this mountain of misery, for months I had to drive to the set of Ron Howard's **The Grinch** at 4:00 a.m. to undergo three hours of makeup to transform me into the head Who of Whoville. There were fake ears, a fake nose, a big rolled wig that looked like a Viennese pastry on my head. We filmed all day on a set covered in fake snow. After the final "Cut!" of the day, I faced another hour and a half to get out of my costume and makeup. It was torturous.

There was an upside, however. There was one lady who I thought was quite fetching. Reader, I flirted with her. But here's the catch: with all the makeup everybody had on, no one knew what anyone else really looked like.

CUT TO: Halfway through the shoot, Ron and his partner Brian Grazer decided to throw a party for the cast and crew. A hump-week party, if you will. It was the first time we would all be in the same place without makeup. To my delight and relief, I discovered that my Who crush was indeed quite lovely in her human form. I invited her out for coffee after that party.

We sat at the Starbucks on Ventura Boulevard and talked and talked and talked. I thought, **This might be okay. Maybe there will be life after Katie. Maybe I will be able to land this ship—** me, not her; I'm the ship.

She asked me where I was from, and I told her about growing up in San Francisco.

"And where are **you** from?" I said in kind.

"My people are Venetian."

"Oh wow, how wonderful. Your family is still there?" I said.

"Yes. I talk to them every night."

"That's so great. Are they in the city of Venice itself, or on the outskirts?"

She smiled as she said, "Oh no, no. Not Venice. Venus."

"What?"

"Venus."

"Venus the planet?"

"Yes."

"I have to go."

I got in my car and drove to my house. I sat in the car in the driveway staring straight ahead for eons. **Venus.**

The next morning, I got a call from Eric Schaeffer, who was writing a film that I would be working on after **The Grinch** wrapped.

"How'd it go last night?"

"Never again," I said.

There was a long pause, and then he said, "That's the title of our movie."

**CUT TO:** Months later, it's nighttime, a sidewalk on the Upper West Side of Manhattan. I was sitting in a director's chair outside Fairway Market next to my costar Jill Clayburgh, as we awaited the next shot. Jill and I had costarred in the ill-fated **Everything's Relative,** and I had been utterly starstruck. We hadn't talked much back then—after all, I had gout—but now we were about to do our first love scene, so I had to say something.

I turned to her and said, "I think you're the best. I think you're astonishing."

Jill burst into tears. "I didn't think you even liked

me." She told me she was afraid of me, and that she thought herself amateurish in comparison to my ability at comedy. I was stunned.

And she was wrong. She is responsible for the funniest scene maybe in the entire history of comedy. During the film, **Never Again,** our characters—two fifty-somethings who have both sworn off romantic relationships—become sexually awakened to each other. Jill's character, at the prompting of her girlfriends, pays a visit to a sex shop to get some toys. In the scene that Jill absolutely killed, she's at home trying on a leather mask and a strap-on dildo when my character unexpectedly pays a visit **with his mother.** Jill runs around the apartment in a frenzy, trying and failing to get the dildo off before opening the door. At the movie's premiere, I sat across from Larry Gelbart, the man who wrote **A Funny Thing Happened on the Way to the Forum** and **M\*A\*S\*H,** and everything else that is funny, and I saw him fall out of his seat laughing. I'm not being metaphoric—he fell out of his seat onto the floor, convulsed with laughter. Jill didn't get to see that because she was in the lobby. She always left the theater before any film she was in began; she couldn't bear to watch herself.

There was another moment that was even funnier and more awkward, but the audience didn't get to see it. We were doing the blocking of a scene in which Jill's teenaged daughter, Lily, in her very first acting role as Jill's character's daughter, walks in on us having sex. The thing is, I hadn't met Lily before. So in she walks, and my face is between her mom's legs. Jill says, "Jeffrey, this is my daughter." A version of the scene appeared in the film, but it could not possibly have captured my utter mortification. Hi, Lily.

Back to the night we sat on the sidewalk talking. That night was the first of many, many nights during which Jill and I became not just friends, but best friends. We had no secrets from each other. I never had a friend like this. I could tell her anything, and she would accept it. She taught me about courage. She confessed that she was ill, a secret she had been keeping for a decade, bluffing her way through the physicals that insurance requires for big-ticket movies so she could keep working, which she did until the very end because she loved it so.

And yet, this was the actress who, after receiving an Academy Award nomination for her role in **An Unmarried Woman** and another a year later for **Starting Over,** stepped back from her career to raise her children, Lily and Michael, out of pure selflessness. I once called her in despair at the end of a film I was working on.

"What do I do now?"

"Go home and raise your children," she said.

When I became engaged to Kasia, I asked Jill to be my best man, but she wasn't feeling well and couldn't make it to the wedding.

In the last year of her life, she faced what was

coming square-on, her children always her focus. One night, we went to dinner at a restaurant where her son, Michael, was a waiter. "Isn't he just the best? Look at him." The pride in that steady, beatific gaze was breathtaking.

Jill was a bit careful with her money, perhaps more than I thought she needed to be. She and her husband, the playwright David Rabe, were very successful, but she drove a used Volvo. I didn't get it. When I asked her about it once, she said, "I have kids to raise and send to college." Her devotion was beautiful.

In the summer of 2010, Kasia and I were on vacation in Southampton out on Long Island, and we'd invited Jill to join us. Jill loved the ocean. If you got her anywhere near water, the clothes came off and she dove in.

One day, Jill and I had taken my kids Gabriel and Evie out for lunch in town. We all had sandwiches, and the kids had ice cream afterward. When the check came, I reached for my wallet.

"I'll get this," I said.

"No, I've got this," Jill said.

I looked at her, and she looked at me, and I knew. Jill's genius as an actor was always in the look. And right then, I knew. There was no time left to worry about money. My dear friend died that November after quietly, courageously facing this illness for more than twenty years. Thank you, Jill.

## <u>HERB</u>

Long before a reality television star moved into the White House, before planes flew into buildings and everyone started shoelessly walking through airports holding plastic baggies with tiny bottles of shampoo, even before the Y2K apocalypse that promised to crash every computer on the planet, before all of that happened and changed everything, I went to a little party at the Statue of Liberty.

It was a balmy night in August 1999, and British journalist Tina Brown and movie mogul Harvey Weinstein had invited 1,000 of their nearest and dearest to celebrate the launch of a new magazine called **Talk.** Everywhere you looked, actors, studio heads, producers, directors, writers, business magnates ate boxed picnic dinners under gaily lit Japanese lanterns and a sky filled with fireworks.

As I waited with a friend for the next ferry to take us across the harbor from Battery Park to join the festivities, I saw my dear Judith Light sitting on a bench with her manager, Herb Hamsher. Far from the crowd, the two sat in silence looking out over the water. Judith was dressed all in black and completely bald.

"Oh no," I said to my friend. "Judith is sick." I hadn't seen her in a while, and now I was afraid to go over there. She and Herb looked so solemn together.

I later found out that Judith had taken over the starring role in a play called **Wit,** in which her character was ravaged by cancer and the follicular devastation of chemo. We still laugh about the mistake I made that night. Or we did, until October 26, 2016, at 5:05 p.m., when Herb left his body and passed into the next realm. Herb was more than Judith's manager and friend; he was the embodiment of support and "attaboy." He was her rock and always at Judith's side. Together they were an unbeatable team and built one of the most solid and brilliant careers around today. It was Herb who prodded Judith to return to her theater roots, a move that has led to two Tony Awards and counting. I like to say, Judith is so good she gets a Tony when she **goes** to the theater. Herb knew that about her before anyone else, including Judith.

The last time I saw Herb, he looked ill, and indeed he was. Herb had brain cancer and his immunotherapy was no longer effective. And yet there he was at the Crosby Street Hotel in New York under the care of his husband, Jonathan Stoller, to support Judith, who was there with me doing press for the third season of **Transparent.** Jonathan had wheeled Herb in to listen to us prattle away about our show. Every once in a while, I would steal a glance over at them. Sometimes, Herb would be smiling. Sometimes, he'd be listening with his eyes closed. He was so very weak. But he was still there, Judith's knight at her side, protecting her to his last breath. He was an inspiration to us all.

Thank you, Herb.

## 10

## Short Answers to the Question "Wow, What's It Like to Be You?"

I think I'm addicted to Ambien.

I make my bed every morning. I love making my bed. It's first and foremost.

I am averse to friends and business reps on the set when we are filming.

I talk to myself, which makes my children laugh at me.

My right hip is titanium. My walk through the TSA sensors at airports sounds like the Baja Marimba Band.

Flossing is one of my favorite pastimes.

When I travel to another city, I rent a car and leave the hotel with no plan other than to get lost.

My oldest daughter, Molly, is smarter than I am—and she knows it.

I cannot fall asleep unless the TV is on.

I cannot fall asleep with the lights off. Hi, American Psychiatric Association.

It is not uncommon for people to think I'm Dr. Phil and thank me for all the good I'm doing.

It is not uncommon for people to think I'm Larry David and thank me for all the good I'm doing.

My first thought in the morning is **Oh, no.**

I have acid reflux and yet will absolutely **not** pass up a good chile relleno or an Indian curry.

I straighten and neaten constantly—the mail pile, chairs, the kids' Legos, books. I have straightened pictures on the walls of other people's houses.

I still play with the satin on my blanket with my thumb and index finger.

I cannot abide emptying the dishwasher.

When my wife is asked if it's laughter 24/7 in our house, she simply rolls her eyes.

I masturbate using pornhub.com. My doctor in Los Angeles says it actually helps the prostate—not

Pornhub, per se, but the actual act of masturbation. Hi, Dr. Biscow.

People think I'm the man on the subway in **Ghost.** That was Vincent Schiavelli, RIP.

I had a bilateral lisp from braces. The first time I asked a girl to go steady, she had no idea what I was saying, and she called me Cliff.

I have a bro-crush on Michael Connelly and his novels. His characters go to the same places in Los Angeles I used to.

I have a huge fear of being fat—Anthony Lane of **The New Yorker,** in his review of the film **Pollock,** called me "the fleshy Jeffrey Tambor."

I hate background music and will complain about it any and every chance I get. Dunkin' Donuts has corporate-mandated Dunkin' Radio in every store. I just don't understand.

I am addicted to:

- Turkey jerky
- Popsicles
- Hanover sourdough pretzels
- Saltines
- Reading

On American Airlines, I take all the biscotti from first class and put it in my carry-on.

On Delta Airlines, I take all the biscotti from first class and put it in my carry-on.

During the opening credits of the film **Never**

**Again,** the camera pans over two old photos of me and my daughter Molly when she was a baby.

I am noise sensitive to a fault. When I stay in a hotel, I change rooms four to five times per visit, even if I'm there only one night. Ask the people at the Langham in London.

I love Van Morrison. I think we might be the same person—he is not a "happy camper."

I cheated on my Physical Science 30 quizzes at San Francisco State. Each week I got the questions from my friend C. Hi, C.!

I went bald when I was eighteen at summer stock. I put whitener in my hair when I was playing an older character and it fell out in clumps.

I love to grocery shop—I am not averse to doing funny walks and false limps in the aisles.

There is nothing quite like a cold hard white peach.

The Church of Scientology keeps trying to find me. They called my New York number two nights ago. If you get a call from the 323 area code, my advice is, let it go to voice mail.

I love to wave at people I don't know while I'm driving.

On a plane ride to L.A., the man sitting next to me tapped me on the shoulder. He didn't say anything, just pointed at his screen. It's me and Jack Black. He went back to watching.

At the screening of **Transparent,** Season Three, at the Toronto International Film Festival, two parents came up to me to tell me about their kid who knew he wanted to transition at the age of four and has successfully done so. More and more, people are approaching me and telling me about their young children transitioning.

There is no better television-watching than the **Great British Bake Off.**

When I stay for any amount of time in New York, I rent a bicycle to get around the city. It is the most efficient system of transportation. Use Sixth Avenue going uptown; go down on Broadway. Avoid the tourists on the bank rent-a-bikes—they have no idea what they're doing.

I eat soup almost every night.

I sometimes sneak into my kids' rooms at night and just sit there watching. Sometimes I smell them. Often, I weep.

I am alive because of daydreaming.

I have a recurring daydream about some anonymous donor leaving me $15 million so my family will be okay after I pass away—might you be that someone?

# The Twelve Most Embarrassing Moments of My Career

My very first commercial audition in New York. My appointment was at five o'clock in the afternoon on a Friday. When I arrived at the casting director's office in lower Manhattan, there was just one person there.

She said, "Your name?"

"Jeffrey Tambor."

"Okay, sign in."

I signed in.

She said, "You're reading for the waiter. Are you ready?"

"I'm reading for the father."

She said, "No, no. You're reading for the waiter."

"I'm sorry, I was told explicitly by my agent, Doris Mantz from ICM"—I was very proud that I was represented by ICM—"I'm reading for the father."

"You're reading for the waiter."

"No, no—"

"Do you know what a casting director is? I am a casting director. I am the top casting director in New York." She said her name and I later found out indeed she was. "I cast this commercial. I select all the names of all the people and I assign them their roles. If they get approved by the client, they get the role. I have a lot of say. And usually what I say goes. If I say, hire this actor or actress, they do. Do you want to read for the waiter?"

"Sure."

So I read the waiter's line about four or five times. It was so over the top, it was as if Boris Karloff entered my body. I couldn't relax. I was horrified. I realized in that moment I had made a huge miscalculation coming to New York.

She said, "Okay."

"That's it?"

"Yeah."

I knew I didn't make it and I turned to leave. When I got to the door, I stopped and turned to her. I had just had my pictures and résumés done at great cost. "Should I leave a picture and résumé?"

"If you must."

## 2

When I was at Wayne State University, I was cast in a production at the Hilberry Classic Theatre of **Becket** as Baron #4. My duty was to walk onstage and announce the death of Becket. The line was, "My lords and ladies, Becket is dead. Long live King Henry." Since this was low-budget repertory theater, actors had to pull their own curtain before making an entrance. The year was 1968 and the Hong Kong flu was making the rounds.

Okay, you have the setup. Here's the humiliation.

I was standing backstage waiting to pull my curtain. Since the play took place in medieval times, my costume was made out of heavy wool spray-painted to look like chain mail. As I stood with my hand on the curtain awaiting my cue, I noticed a little growling in my stomach. **Must be a little gas from that pastrami I had at lunch at Teddy's.** I looked to my left. I looked to my right. Coast was clear. **I'll just expel that before I walk on.** With the gentlest of flexed abdominal muscles to pass the gas, I utterly and completely befouled myself just as I heard my cue: "Here comes Baron #4!"

I pulled my curtain and walked, **skloosh skloosh skloosh,** onto the stage and said, "My lords and ladies, Becket is dead!" **Skloosh skloosh skloosh.** "Long live King Henry!"

It was all going fine, but as I passed each cast member, a horrified look would pass over each face. Also, as this was not a very large theater, I quickly noticed that the first couple of rows in the audience were becoming restive during my short speech. I turned to make my exit. **Skloosh skloosh skloosh.** And I pulled the curtain on Embarrassing Moment **Number Two.**

**3**

A Bounce commercial became a defining moment in my life. All I had to say was, "Hey, my socks don't cling."

I couldn't do it.

I said, "You know, my socks don't cling."

Director said, "It's 'hey.'"

I said, "You know, my socks don't cling."

"Try again."

"You know a funny thing about socks."

"Again."

"Hey, my socks . . . I'm sorry, what's the line?"

I was sweating so much they had blow dryers pointed at my armpits.

A producer yelled out, "How many fucking actors in this city?"

The crew is muttering, "What the fuck. Let us go home, man, just say the words."

You have to understand, an eight-year-old had just gone before me, and he said the line just fine. There was a grandma actress who had done it. I could not do it.

Eventually, hours later, I got through it. I took the F train home to Brooklyn. I walked fifteen minutes from Jay Street Borough Hall to our house on Dean Street. I walked up the four flights to our apartment. I walked in. My wife said, "How did it go?"

I cried for the next six hours.

**4**

One night during the Ford administration, I was doing a speech in a performance of Bertolt Brecht's **The Visions of Simone Machard** at the Milwaukee Repertory Theater in front of a subscription audience. These are the most dedicated audiences, as they buy tickets to the whole season without even knowing what is going to be performed.

I was center stage, the spotlight was on me, when I heard a rustle from the audience. It happens, no big deal. I kept going.

Then I heard, "Liberté, egalité, fraternité." **The French national motto? What the fuck?**

I stopped the play. I motioned to everyone on-stage to stop. I walked to the front of the stage and said, "Who's talking?"

Not a peep from the audience. After a beat, we went on with the show. We found out later the man had had some sort of "episode," but he'd enjoyed the hell out of the show.

**5**

While I was an undergraduate at San Francisco State, it was mandatory in the theater program to take classes in makeup, sound, stage management, and lighting. I was fine with all of it, except lighting. The professor was a very nice man, although I think they may have invented the OCD diagnosis in his honor. Every pencil on his desk was sharpened to the exact same degree and length. He was humorless, but dedicated to lighting.

To pass the class, students had to climb an A-frame ladder nearly three stories high to put gels in the Fresnel and ellipsoidal lights. Someone would move the ladder while you were on it to get you to the next set of lights.

There are a lot of things I can do—bake bread, do crossword puzzles, drive—but heights and me, we don't get along.

CUT TO: The day it was my turn to go up the

ladder. It took me forty-five minutes to get to the top. When I was up there, I had to straddle it while someone moved me light to light.

I began screaming, "Get me down! Get me down! Get me down! Fuck this! I don't care if I flunk! Get me down!" I was given an A in the course on the solemn promise that I would never go near a lighting instrument again. I have kept my promise.

## 6

In 1978 I was invited to audition for a reunion of the storied TV Western **Gunsmoke,** starring James Arness.

I drove up to the gate at Paramount and told the guard, "I have a meeting."

He said, "You don't have a meeting. You have an audition."

I walked in. "We're very honored to have you." I was somewhat well known by then. The director explained the part was a regular guy in town. "Would you mind reading the line? Kick it around a little?"

"Kick it around" is a euphemism for "audition."

I started reading my part, and it came out Irish.

The director said, "Hold on. Let me say again how honored we are to have you. But he's not Irish."

I said, "Oh, I know."

"Okay. Because it's sounding a little Irish. Let's go again."

I did it again.

"It's still coming out Irish."

"I know. I can't control it." It was like I had been possessed by Sean O'Casey. I had no idea what had happened to me.

I did it a couple more times and it came out **more** Irish.

Finally, the director said, "Well, okay. We'll think about this."

They called my agent and said, "Is Jeffrey all right?"

In our production of **Julius Caesar** at the Hilberry Rep in Detroit, I played the title character and the wonderful Fred Coffin played one of the guys who assassinated me. The staging of the assassination was done beautifully. The actors surrounding me when I was stabbed repeatedly had these enema bags under their armpits filled with stage blood. They would squeeze their arms and the blood would spray onto my nice white costume.

One night, the enema bag got stuck under Fred Coffin's armpit, and he went into this wild chicken dance in front of me trying to get the blood to come out. The more he tried to get the blood out, the more his elbow flapped, and the more I laughed. They all backed away and I fell to the ground as clean as a whistle.

On the nights the blood worked, I had a different problem. It turned out that I was allergic to the fake blood, so I would balloon up. When the scene was done and I left the stage, me and my giant face would go smoke a cigarette and wait for curtain call. The audience had no idea who I was when I came out to take a bow.

**8**

Lest you think that all my embarrassing moments happened in remote theaters in front of small audiences, allow me to share one from my Broadway debut in **Sly Fox.** It was a Sunday matinee, and I was doing a scene with the great Jack Gilford. What you need to know is that we had a rotating set for this production, which meant that while you were doing one scene, the stage crew was setting up the next one in the blacked-out part. The whole thing was built on a 360-degree rotating disk, so at the end of a scene, the whole set rotated and the actors were already in place for the next one.

So this one Sunday, we had a different crew than we usually had. As the lights went down on the scene I was doing with Jack, the crew turned the set the wrong way. The roof of the set fell on my head in front of the audience, and I fell to the ground. The audience gasped. They stopped the show and rang down the curtain. The house lights came on. I was still on the floor. I saw blood. **Am I alive or dead?** I heard Jack Gilford say, "Oh my God! He's dead!" **I must be dead.**

My wig saved my life. I was just thirty-two years old, but I was already bald, so I had to wear a toupee for my role in the play. Members of the crew came over to me and dabbed the blood off my face.

When I realized I was still alive, I said, "Let's finish it." There were only two scenes left, maybe twenty minutes. "I can do it. I can do it."

In their haste and compassion, they had shoved about fifty tissues underneath the toupee to stanch the bleeding from my head. So when the lights came up and we resumed the play, my head had assumed a large egg shape. I had no idea I looked ridiculous. What I did know is that somber requiem quickly changed to a riot of giggling and farting and snorting. I still didn't know what everyone was laughing at, and I became increasingly furious. How dare they?

I got a great ovation at the end of the performance that night, and then someone took me to Lenox Hill Hospital to get my scalp stitched up and some pain meds.

My wife met me in the emergency room to take me home, but there was an actors benefit for a play called **The Gin Game** with the legendary Hume Cronyn and Jessica Tandy. An actors benefit is one of the most extraordinary events imaginable because the theater community is one of the most heartfelt communities going. It's hard to do Broadway, it takes sacrifice; so if you do Broadway, you've really earned your bones. When Joyce said, "You have to go home," I said, "We're going to the benefit."

I won the argument and we headed off to the event. I was feeling a little sorry for myself and out of sorts, because I was unhappy with how the cast had laughed at me. (I still didn't know about the tissues under my toupee.)

We took our seats, and the lights dimmed. There was a bare stage with a table and two chairs, and in place were Jessica Tandy and Hume Cronyn. They got an ovation right away and it lasted for at least five minutes. They were actors' actors, and the audience went crazy. The play was the most artful and nuanced performance you could imagine. Here I was with my head throbbing, and it was an extraordinary moment.

That Monday after my accident and after the actors benefit, the lawyer for the Shuberts came to my apartment on Seventy-First Street. He asked me if I was going to sue for damages.

"I probably should, as it was sheer negligence and I could have died."

"True."

"But I'm afraid I would never work in a Shubert theater again."

"Any Shubert or any other theater on Broadway," he corrected me.

I signed the release that said I wouldn't sue them, but I kept the story.

**9**

The worst note I ever got in the theater was a hand-written note left on the stage with my name on it after a rehearsal of George Bernard Shaw's **Major Barbara:** "Don't cross your legs in the Third Act. No one likes to see a fat thigh."

**10**

I was fortunate to appear in the 1976 New York Shakespeare Festival production of **Measure for Measure** directed by John Pasquin and starring Meryl Streep, her then boyfriend John Cazale, Sam Waterston, and my dear friend Judith Light. I played Elbow, who is described as "a simple constable." At the curtain call, when it was my turn, I walked out to the center of the stage to take a bow. There was a man standing in the fifth row of the audience. **How odd. Standing ovation?** He wasn't applauding, his hands were at his sides. As I started to take my bow, he cupped his hands to his mouth and shouted, "Boo!" It wasn't enough to sit and boo me, he had to stand to make the criticism as severe as he could. I still don't know what his problem was. Everyone else was applauding.

**11**

When I first moved to Los Angeles, there was an agent at ICM I was trying to get to sign me. When I called him on the phone, he would say, "Hey, how you doing, hot ticket?" When I saw him in his office, he would say, "Hey, hot ticket!" Having a big shot Hollywood agent call me "hot ticket" was as good as an "attaboy" any day. One day as I was leaving his office, bursting with pride at my special status in this revered man's eyes, another actor said, "He calls you that because he can't remember your name."

**12**

During a scene with Al Pacino in **And Justice for All,** I had my first close-up. When Norman Jewison yelled, "Action!," Al smooshed his face up against the side of the camera. I didn't know he was supposed to do that, so that my eyes would be looking as nearly into the camera as possible. I thought he was goofing around, and I laughed. At Al Pacino.

# Do It Badly, or Let's Wreck It

I was having dinner with my friend Milton Katselas, the brilliant acting teacher, at a steakhouse in L.A. I'd been studying with him for a while, and we were becoming friends.

"What's going on?" That was always his opening salvo when he knew something was going on with me.

"I'm good," I lied.

"What's going on?"

"Everything feels off. I feel different when I act. I feel, I don't know—constricted."

"What's that?" he said through a mouthful of porterhouse.

"I'm getting tighter and tighter in my acting." That morning, I'd shot an episode of **Hill Street Blues** in Studio City. I was playing Judge Wachtel. I was done early, so I changed my clothes in my dressing room and went for my usual ten-mile run. While running, I caught myself going over and over the script, and running lines—not on tomorrow's work but from the scene I'd just shot. I stopped dead in my tracks. **What the fuck is going on? Something is way, way wrong.**

"The eyes are on you," Milton said, reaching for the French fries.

"What?"

"The eyes are on you."

What Milton was casually saying was something that people in the psychology world have been touting for years—that which is observed changes. Psychologists know that the observed will change to meet the expectations of the observer.

Anyway, he was right. By the mid-1980s, I had a recurring role on a top television show, and people were noticing me—and I noticed them noticing.

Under that gaze, I became not myself but this actor with this built-in expectancy. It's what happened when I first did **Sly Fox** in front of Larry Gelbart. "Wait till you see the kid" ruined me. I was trying to be perfect to impress people, but that's not where the "good stuff," as they say, comes from. To find your purpose—or your "primary reason," as George Saunders so aptly describes it, or as we used to say in the '60s, your "thing"—I believe you first must be willing to wreck it.

The author Henry Miller said his teacher told him he knew what he sounded like when Miller tried to write well, but what did it sound like when he tried to do it badly? And that's when Henry Miller said he found his "voice." Philip Roth (another literary "crush") said he wrote 100 pages of a new novel and then he wrote one sentence that threw him for a loop. That sentence became the idea, or the "new" idea, for the novel, and that page became his new page one. When asked what he did with the previously written 100 pages, he said, "I threw them out, and hoped to never see them again." My beloved Anne Lamott says a writer must have their "shitty first drafts."

I believe this: errors are essential and need to be welcomed. They are the opposite of perfection and yet can lead to genius and revelation. "I don't know" is what Robert Frost was talking about when he wrote of the marvelous "road less traveled."

Recently I read of a CEO of a very successful company, who says this to his people:

**You will not be fired here for making mistakes.**
**You will be fired here for not making mistakes.**
**I want 50 percent errors.**
**I want quick decisions.**
**I want innovation.**
**I want you to make big-ass mistakes.**

That's why we invented the pencil, because there's an eraser.

And part of it is accepting your story. Every morning I get up, the "story" is right there waiting for me. I call the story "the vultures"—there they are perched on the edge of the bed, awaiting me.

**Good morning, Beppy! Shh, shh, shh,** one vulture says.

The other vulture says, **Good morning, Stinky! How are you? You were snoring last night. I think you're borderline sleep apnea. You should probably get that checked out. And by the way, we're going to be with you all day, you piece of shit.**

The vultures are with me at the awards ceremony when I'm sitting at table 236 way in the back of the theater. When my name is called, the vultures say,

**Hey, Cleff. We're going to accompany you to the stage to accept your Golden Globe.**

**Shhhhhhh** as the audience applauds.

**Shtick drek** as the golden statuette is placed into my hands.

I notice that when my twins are playing with their Legos, they will fasten piece upon piece, building higher and higher, delighting in the shape and different colors and making it go to the ceiling. Then, when it is all done and in place—**WHACK!**—they destroy it, fast, loudly, and with exuberance. They not only have joy in creating something, but also in destroying it so they can get on to the next.

I make it a point to get lost when I go to a new city. I'll walk out of my hotel, get in the rental car, and just "get lost." Years ago I was in Lisbon, Portugal, with my girlfriend, and I suggested we go explore without plans, and we did indeed get lost. We drove and drove, and then on the horizon, this Alhambra appeared, a lost, ancient city, beautiful and old with big gates. While we were there, someone told us to have the stone soup at the local restaurant. They served it cold and put a hot stone in it to heat it, and it was delicious. I had never tasted anything quite like it.

After our lunch, we resumed driving and took a random left turn off the highway. We went down this twisty unpaved road, and suddenly there appeared a circus. It was midafternoon, so there were no customers, just empty tents and animals sleeping in their cages. It was like a dream. We went into a trailer and found a performer in his tights and wife-beater sitting with his beautiful wife getting ready for a performance. This trailer was their dressing room, and they had their little black-and-white TV on. They recognized me immediately: "Ah, Mr. Roper." The couple showed us around the circus grounds that magical afternoon. All this from getting "lost."

Years ago during rehearsals for a production of **The Two Gentlemen of Verona** at the Milwaukee Rep, the director stopped us and said, "Do what you want. Let's have fun with this." He wasn't a loosey-goosey director like that—he was brilliant. So Jim Baker dragged me around the stage while I held on to his leg as we said our Shakespearean lines, yelling them, overacting, doing it so very badly. We broke all the Elizabethan and American stagecraft rules, and everybody fell out of their seats laughing. People in the rehearsal room were gasping. The play just lifted and lifted and became very funny and accessible.

"Okay, okay, that's enough," the director said. "Let's return to the text."

We then returned to verse, but the production caught fire from that moment on. All from doing it wrong.

In movies and television, the director might have you do many takes of a scene until it's done, and then say, "Now do one for yourself." Inevitably—

ask any actor—that's the take that's full of play and creativity and joy and is the one that has the most freedom and life. On the **Transparent** set, Jill Soloway starts us with that take. That is, indeed, our premise.

Dopamine and serotonin flow through the body when you play. It makes you joyful and fearless. When you submit to the eyes being on you, the work ceases to be play and becomes something else, something rigid, something **expected.**

You have to kill expectancy. Because the vultures? That's what they eat for breakfast.

## Dailies

"Y̶ou got the part," my agent said over the phone.

"I know I got it. We already talked about it."

"No, no, not **The Ropers.** You got **And Justice for All.**"

Oh. My. God.

When I was called in to read for a role in this new Al Pacino film—and Al was just coming off the mega success of **The Godfather** and had assumed superstar status—I was stunned. I had a few things going against me: 1) Norman Jewison, who was directing the film and was also a producer, had already settled on another actor; 2) I had never done a film before; and 3) My agent warned me not to let on that I was bald. Norman did not want any hair-impaired actors, I was warned, because the character has to shave his head in the movie. I wore the **Sly Fox** wig to the audition.

Upon entering the room I immediately copped to it and announced, "I'm wearing a wig."

I saw the casting director slap his palm to his forehead in the back of the room. And then: when I sat down to read, Norman was on the left, and his producing partner Patrick Palmer was on the right.

"Are you nervous?" Norman asked. I said I was. "You want a cigarette?"

Norman offered his pack of Merits, and Patrick offered a Lucky Strike. I said, "Give me the kind that killed Nat King Cole." They looked at each other, and I kind of knew I had the role. Even so, it was a shock to get the official call.

My wife wasn't at home that day, and I had no one else to tell, so I got on my bicycle and rode all over

New York. I stopped random people on the street to tell them, and people were actually interested!

Starting the next day, Al would pick me up and we'd get to work. I was under his tutelage. I think it was his methodology, but I also think I was a newbie with a capital New and he was going to make sure I didn't fuck it up. We were both playing lawyers in the film, and we wanted to learn the rudiments of what a trial looks like, where the lawyers stand and what they do. The first thing we did was go over to the courthouse in downtown Brooklyn to watch. The only thing is, when Al Pacino sits in a courtroom, it morphs into something else. The judge was sitting up straight and being very orotund in his pronouncements, the lawyers seemed to be preening, and the court stenographer was all but pole dancing. They were all, in fact, acting.

First on the docket that day was a larceny case, I believe: someone had stolen a tortoise from a zoo. The judge was attempting to assize the penalty.

Where is tortoise theft in the penal code? The judge decided that the value of said tortoise would be determined by the age of the tortoise, so, like assessing the age of a tree, they were counting the rings on the shell.

Every day we did something to prepare for our roles. We would be at lunch and Al would be talking about something, and all of a sudden he'd be doing the scene. One minute he was ordering the lentil soup, and the next he was saying, "Well, you know, Jay . . ." My new teacher was implicitly saying, there was no space between life and the scene.

When shooting began, we went down to Baltimore. We ran our scenes in every restaurant, cafeteria, and taxi in that city. I didn't have any scenes on the first day of shooting, but I went to the set to watch. I was "up" the next day. (Please see "The Twelve Most Embarrassing Moments of My Career," page 139, to find out how that went.)

The following day, Al called over to my hotel—I was staying downtown at a seedy place, and he was in a nice hotel across town—and said, "Do you want to come to dailies?"

"Sure."

As I was leaving my room, I ran into Jack Warden, who was staying in the same hotel as I. It was December, and Jack had a habit of playing Nat King Cole's "Have Yourself a Merry Little Christmas" over and over again on the jukebox in the hotel bar.

"Hey, where you going?" he said.

"I'm going to dailies," I said.

"You sure you want to do that?"

"Yeah, yeah, I do."

"Have you ever been to dailies?" Jack said.

"Nope, first time. Al just asked me to go."

"Lemme ask you a question."

"Yeah?"

"What if you don't like 'em?"

I shrugged. I walked over to the nice hotel where Al and Norman were staying.

I was interested to see how Al watched dailies. When he talked about the scene, he referred to his character rather than to himself. "I like when he . . ." I thought that was brilliant. He was able to remove himself from the picture.

I, alas, was not a "he." I was definitely an "I."

I took my seat. The vultures took theirs on either side of me. I watched my scene, and every single take was horrifying. I hated every aspect of my performance. **Shtick drek, shtick drek. Shhh shhh, they'll take it away from you.** David Siegel, who was Al's driver and assistant at the time (he's a big producer now and his daughter works in the **Transparent** office), had to drive me around the city of Baltimore until four in the morning while I contemplated not only quitting the movie, but quitting acting altogether.

It turned out that I wasn't entirely wrong, and we did reshoot my scene. But I learned my lesson. I do not look at dailies, or the finished product, if I can help it. When I look at myself in the mirror in the morning, I look a little bald. But when I see myself onscreen? Oh My God.

Some people can look at themselves with a clear eye, but not me. I love it between "Action" and "Cut," and then I have to walk away.

If it were done
When 'tis done
Then 'twere **well**
It were done quickly

Hi, Al.

## 14

## You Must Fail

There is no such thing as a straight line to success, in life, in love, or in career. You're going to fuck up somewhere along the way. You might make a bad decision, a stupid choice, an ill-informed move. You might choose to do something good, but for the wrong reason. You might choose something bad for the right reason.

When I was a kid, I appeared in a school talent show in blackface to lip-sync an Al Jolson number, then walked offstage the wrong way into a closet, where I stayed for the entire show, knowing full well all the kids in the audience knew what I had done and could see the shut door of the darkened closet. As failures go, not huge, but I still get a little hot in the cheeks remembering it.

Those kinds of failures, you recover from. You apologize, atone, whatever is called for, and move on, or not.

Six years ago, I let myself down. I mean, **down.** The universe whispered in my ear, "Go fuck yourself," and I did. I had seen a production of the musical **La Cage aux Folles** in L.A. with Keene Curtis, and I wasn't a fan. Of the book or the music. So obviously when my agent called to ask if I'd like to take over the role of Georges, then being played by Kelsey Grammer on Broadway, I said yes.

Although I had done theater for years, I'd never been in a musical. It had been one of my dreams since I was a little kid, when I used to go to the audiovisual room in the library and watch Donald O'Connor sing and dance "Make 'Em Laugh" in **Singin' in the Rain** and listen to Ethel Merman in **Gypsy.** I wanted to put a musical on my résumé before I shuffled off this mortal coil and joined my friend on Venus.

Frankly, none of this explains why I said yes to this show. Nothing explains it.

The show had a storied history; it had been running off and on in one guise or another for years. Gene Barry had been in one incarnation of it, and it had been enormously successful for Harvey Fierstein, who'd written the book, and the producers, Barry and Fran Weissler.

They asked me, "Do you want to come see the show?" I didn't go. The fucking of myself was nearly complete.

I went to my singing lessons, I listened to the music, I prepared the text. I was subletting Helen Hunt's apartment on West Eighty-Sixth Street during the run. Every day they'd send someone over to run lines with me.

I went to the table read, and I killed. I murdered. People went nuts. Harvey tweeted his praise of my performance at the table read. And then it was all downhill from there. I lost my mojo. And the universe smelled weakness the way sharks smell blood.

Nobody in the production told me that:

1. There would be no four full weeks of rehearsal, as is customary.
2. The director would not be present for the first week and a half of the rehearsals; only the stage manager, whom I adored.
3. The choreographer would not be present; I was told she was pregnant and near delivery.

4. I had to beg to get one rehearsal with the
   orchestra before I appeared in front of an audience. They hadn't planned to give me that
   opportunity, and I believe they thought it
   quite pushy of me to ask.

Harvey kept saying in his rasp: "Get on the train."
To this day, I have no idea what he was talking
about, nor indeed where this particular train was. I
think it ran directly up my own ass.

On the night of my first preview performance,
I got to my dressing room after dinner to find
presents and flowers and notes declaring, "Happy
Opening!"

What. The. Fuck?

Normally you get three to four weeks of previews,
to get acclimated to the role and the performance.
The audience knows there may be a few glitches or
changes in a preview. Critics don't review previews.
Turns out, this was no preview. This was indeed
opening night.

There were no critics in attendance, but there
were people sitting in the front tables, which had
been arranged cabaret-style, very expensive seats,
and they were expecting to get their money's worth.
I didn't have the role down. I didn't have enough rehearsal. Those people in the front seats had shelled
out a fortune to see me flail. And I mean flail with
a capital FLAIL.

After the first night, everyone welcomed me downstairs in the theater. One of the producers came into my dressing room and said, "Congratulations." I fell into his arms and wept as copiously as I had after visiting Auschwitz. Later, another producer's wife alcoholically whispered into my ear, "You're better than he was."

This just in—I was **not** better than nor even near or adjacent to Kelsey. I was, however, dreadful.

I wasn't kidding myself. I was sixty-five years old, it was eight shows a week, and I wasn't on top of it. I was performing in a show I didn't like before I was ready, and you can't learn like that. My knees started to go, my hips started to go, my back started to go. And my confidence was in Topeka. During every performance, I was awash in sweat. My character wears a wig, but Harvey and the director had the idea of my taking the wig off ten or fifteen minutes in and doing the rest of it bald. I think the audience couldn't get used to that; they didn't laugh or applaud when I did it. The producers didn't like it.

The theater is a very small, cloistered world. Musical theater is even smaller. And I was a total outsider. The vultures and I would get to the theater each day and shake with dread as I wrote my name on the sign-in sheet.

The cherry on the top of this fuck sundae was the rumor mill.

I would wander around backstage, in my dressing room, in the halls, muttering to myself: "I don't know why I'm in this show. What am I doing? Oh my God!" As I said good night to cast and crew, I'd say, "I hope I see you tomorrow."

I suspect someone was "sending" everything I said up the line. People were starting to wonder aloud, "Is he coming in?"

The cast had been doing the show for so long, they were in the groove, and I couldn't get near it. Even though Harvey had joined the production at the same time I did, it was his show; he had written it. I never knew whom I'd be playing against. They had this platooning system for some of the characters, so one night you'd be playing opposite one actor, and the next someone completely different. I was trying to master my lines and finding myself face-to-face with a stranger. It was another thing no one had told me.

One performance, yet another producer came to my dressing room and said, "You must be feeling very fragile today." It was the afternoon my wife and two older kids came to the show. In fact, it was one of my best performances, and went very well. I found out later there was a reporter from the **New York Post** in attendance. He broke the rule about not pre-reviewing, and he let me have it. "Tambor's struggling. And he knows it."

I got a note from my agent the next day. "They're very afraid that you're leaving the show. Are you leaving the show? If so, they don't want you to go on tonight. They want to go with the understudy."

"What, no, I'm not leaving." But clearly they were taking a defensive posture in case I was.

On a Wednesday night, I was in the middle of a patter song in Act Two and I flubbed a line. I had struggled with the lyrics, so I'd written on every surface, desk, lamp on the set. I flubbed anyway. And once you flub a line in a patter, you're in trouble. I think I made up some words. Allyce Beasley, who was onstage with me at the time, traded a look with Harvey while I died. They laughed.

I finished the song and walked offstage. As I passed the stage manager, I said, "See me in my dressing room after the show."

When she came down, I said, "Call management."

"Jeffrey."

"Call management."

She got him on the phone.

"I'm out," I told him.

"Are you sure?"

I don't think he was heartbroken. I'm sure people were calling Jerry Herman, the composer, and saying, "A crime is being perpetrated." And indeed it was.

So I left.

I had the driver drive me around Manhattan for a long time. I called my manager. I called my agent. I had never felt alone like that before. I mean, there's alone, and there's **alone.** When I finally walked in my house, Kasia was devastated. She's a very by-the-bootstraps kind of person. If there's a problem, you fix it.

I didn't sleep at all that night. The next day, I walked around in a fog. I lived in that fog for weeks. As far as the press was concerned, I left due to hip problems. The brief **Times** article about my departure seemed more interested in Kelsey's upcoming fourth wedding.

I went out to L.A. for the opening of **Paul,** a film in which I had a very small part. I made my wonderful agent Leslie Siebert sit with me. She held my hand. I'd done some serious reputation damage back East, but in L.A. no one was thinking about **La Cage aux Folles.** She tried to convince me my career was not over.

I next saw Harvey at the opening for the wonderful Audra McDonald's Billie Holiday show. I'd had a feeling driving into the city from my home in Westchester that I would run into him, and there he was, resplendent and looking rather good. He was standing next to the lead from **Kinky Boots,** his Broadway show. I walked up to Harvey and said, "I'd love to have lunch with you." The lunch never happened, but what I wanted to say was, "I'm sorry for the enormous problem that I caused." I did write that to him. It was the least I could do, considering they'd had to go back into rehearsal, find a permanent replacement. But the show sputtered and closed.

In retrospect, I should never have taken the role. Getting out of it, I was making a run for my life. I could have finished the run, I could have made it through, but I found myself thinking, **If it were done, when 'tis done, then 'twere** well **it were done quickly.** Macbeth and I left the building.

**CUT TO:** Not long ago, I was shopping in DeCicco's, my local grocery. I was in the produce section, and I caught a glimpse of something familiar out of the corner of my eye. **Harvey? That can't be Harvey. Just keep pushing your shopping cart, Jeffrey.**

In the next aisle, I think I see him again. In the next, **That's Harvey's back. I know it.**

He wasn't making a move, so I thought, **Fuck it**, and I walked over. "Hi, Harvey. What are you doing here?"

"Hi, Jeffrey," he said in that inimitable rasp that's part yenta and part Indy 500.

We stopped our carts and chatted, but not really making any eye contact.

"There's the Melba toast."

"Oh, here's that instant Cream of Wheat I've always wanted to try."

We pushed our carts and continued with this noncommittal conversation. He was living in Ridgefield. I told him I had a Ridgefield library card.

It was so Jewish, two Jewish boys shopping and reforming their lives through shopping. He congratulated me on the Golden Globe.

Finally, at the checkout, I said, "It was really good seeing you."

I still feel shame about leaving the show like I did. It was an amateur move. And it hurt a lot of people. And no matter how hard I try, I cannot figure out why I said yes.

My wife gave me a coffee cup this Hanukkah. It says, LET IT GO—and she hadn't even read this chapter.

## 15

## In Thrall

To be in thrall is to be consumed by the need to please, the need to have people like you and to like your work. It is as though you are under a spell.

That is certainly how it felt to me in the early

days of my career as a young actor. I was always worried about doing it right, having the right costume, the right prop, the right timing, the right entrance, the right exit. Would the audience like me? Would the director like me? Being in thrall to someone or something is death to spontaneity and invention. And allegiance to its rules is dangerous. Mediocrity is close by.

When I was doing **Sly Fox** on Broadway, there was a man with a white beard and wearing a safari jacket who came backstage after a performance to say hello to George C. Scott and Héctor Elizondo. There was something about him that drew my attention. Afterward, I said to Héctor, "Who's that guy?"

"That's Milton Katselas. He's a character."

Milton was a renowned theater and film director who had received a Tony nomination for **Butterflies Are Free,** which he also directed for the big-screen version starring Goldie Hawn. He had studied with Lee Strasberg at the famed Actors Studio in New York and worked closely with the great director Elia Kazan. In 1978 he founded the Beverly Hills Playhouse, where he taught some of the biggest heavy hitters in the business.

CUT TO: A few years later, I noticed that some of my actor friends were talking about a class they took Saturday mornings with the same Milton Katselas. One was Craig T. Nelson, whom I'd worked with in **And Justice for All.** Another was Valerie

Curtin, who had cowritten the film with her then husband and writing partner, Barry Levinson.

One Saturday, I decided to check it out. I made my way down to the Zephyr Theatre on Melrose Avenue in Hollywood. The Zephyr was this little ninety-nine-seat theater in the back of an alley. The stage was surrounded on three sides by seats where the class assembled, waiting for Milton. I looked around and noted some of the major-league talent in this room: Doris Roberts, Jessica Walter, Tony Lo Bianco, Tyne Daly.

Milton arrived on crutches and attended on both sides by helpers as he made his way to the front row. The helpers settled him into his seat and brought another chair for him to prop up his leg.

"What happened to his leg?" I whispered to the student sitting next to me. She gave me a stern look that seemed to say one didn't ask questions about Milton.

When I looked back down toward the front row, Milton was talking to the veteran television actor James Farentino. Quickly, the conversation grew heated—something about theater policy—and then they were yelling at each other. Milton kept saying, "No, no, I don't agree with you, Jimmy." It was quite an introduction—first the grand entrance on crutches and then an argument with one of Hollywood's most famous leading men.

Then class began. I didn't love the work the actors were doing in the first scenes Milton had assigned, but after each one, they would step to the edge of the stage and sit down. Milton would say, "Anything you want to say?"

The actor would do a short exegesis of his approach or concerns, and then Milton would look at his legal pad and begin his critique. What I remember is that the critique was so much better than the scenes. His notes were spot-on—educational, often funny, and quite inspiring. He was indeed a master teacher.

After he gave each note, he would draw a line through it with a pencil. I can still hear the scratch of that pencil on the paper as he did so. What I didn't know was that I was going to hear that scratch of pencil on pad for the next twenty years.

I walked up to him after class to introduce myself and pay my respects. He said, "I know who you are. Come back next week. Don't worry about signing up. Just come back."

The next week, I went back. And the next. And the next. I was mesmerized by the critiques he gave, which were as much about life as about acting.

About two months in, I was ready to do a scene. I brought a copy of the poem "Birches" by Robert Frost. I didn't tell anyone I was going to read it, but when I arrived in class, a bit late that day, he said, "We're going to do some work today, and then Jeffrey is going to read from Robert Frost's 'Birches.'" I have no idea how he knew. Anyway, one person did a scene and got a critique, then another person did a scene and got a critique, and then I was up. I sat on the edge of the stage, put on my glasses, and read the poem in my basso-important-Jeffrey voice. When I was done, Milton stepped over to me and gave me my critique.

"You do not need to study here," he said. "You're already a fine actor. You know what you're doing. But, if you should decide to study here, this is what we would work on. You ready?"

I nodded.

"You're a good boy," he said. "You're a director's dream."

"What do you mean?"

"You're a good boy," he said. "You're the first one off book. You're the first one to rehearsal. You like to please people. That's a good thing, and a bad thing."

He had me nailed. No one had ever said that to me.

"Bring this back next week."

The whole week, I kept fulminating. **What am I going to do? What am I going to do?** I was in a play at the time, and I went to the property master and said, "Do you have a gun?" I have no idea why I said this. He gave me a prop gun that had no chamber, and the gun hole (who says "gun hole"?) was blocked. I didn't work on the poem at all.

The following Saturday, I went to class and sat in the theater with the other students. Milton arrived and took his seat.

The girl sitting next to me had her back somewhat turned to me, as though I wasn't important
enough to sit near her. I had no idea who she was. I
waited and waited and waited until finally Milton
said, "And now Jeffrey will do 'Birches.'"

I asked the great Doris Roberts, who played the
mother in **Everybody Loves Raymond,** and two
or three other people to come up onstage. I set it
up like a casting session, with the other actors sitting behind a desk, and I was there for an audition.
There was a piano onstage. I didn't tell them anything else.

I knocked on the door, and Doris said, "Come in."

I walked in and began to read "Birches." I did
it with a lisp. When I had a lisp as a young person, it had been a point of great derision. Everyone
had always laughed at my lisp. And as soon as I
started to recite the poem, they started to laugh, as
I knew they would. That's when I pulled my gun
and pointed it at them. Then I pointed it at my head.
Trish Van Devere, who was married to George C.
Scott, was in the third or fourth row and she stood
up and said, "Don't do it, Jeffrey!"

I walked over to the piano and said, "Do you
mind if I play?"

They were all thrown. Doris was crying. Everybody was crying. I sat down at the piano and began
to sing "Feelings," still with the lisp but in a sweet
voice. I don't know how to play the piano, so my

playing was just **plonk plonk plonk** as I pounded the keys. It was madness. People were laughing.

And then I stopped playing and finished my reading of the poem, which when filtered through all the mayhem and emotion, boiled down to this:

**I'd like to get away from Earth a while**
**And then come back to it and begin over.**
**May no fate willfully misunderstand me**
**And half grant what I wish and snatch me**
**Away**
**Not to return.**
**Earth's the right place for**
**Love**

And there was silence and tears.

I do not remember Milton's critique. But I remember while he was talking to me that he kept turning to look at someone in the back row who was visiting the class, as though to say, "You see? You see?" I knew it was good, whatever was happening.

During the break, the visitor walked up to me and said, "Do you want to know what Milton just said to me? 'That's Marlon. Marlon acts like that.'" Marlon Brando was one of Milton's heroes. Hell, Marlon Brando was everybody's hero. That first critique from the previous week changed my life. I did it badly. The good boy was vanquished.

I didn't have to study anymore after that, but I went

to that Saturday class from 9:30 a.m. to 1:00 p.m. for the next twenty years. Eventually, Milton had so many classes to teach during the week, he couldn't do them all, and he asked me to teach those. Some weeks, I taught Monday and Wednesday; others, I taught Tuesday and Thursday. I still have actors coming up to me to this day introducing themselves to me with their name and then "Tuesday/Thursday" or "Monday/Wednesday."

Over time, the class became reality, and what happened outside of class wasn't. You didn't work to improve your acting for the films and plays you were doing, you worked to be successful for the class, for Milton. After I did a reading, he would sidle up to me and say, "You're one fuck of an actor." It was the biggest "attaboy" an actor could have gotten. I ate it up.

He also claimed part of your life outside of class. After the Saturday class, a small group of us—all men—were invited to his house for lunch and to hang out, maybe watch a basketball game on television. It was not an invitation one could refuse. Friday nights, he would take a group of hangers-on out for dinner. There were so many hangers-on, and I became the president of them. I was Milton's right-hand man.

Here's the irony: the one thing he said I needed to work on as an actor was breaking out of being a good boy, but here I was being a good boy for him, living to please him. I gave up my marriage to Katie, one of the most charming and wonderful people in the world, for him. I stopped speaking to my daughter Molly for a while because Milton told me, "Don't bring her around." (I cringe as I write this. To have such cowardice about my own child; it was as if I were possessed.)

**CUT TO:** I was in New York filming **Meet Joe Black.** I had no girlfriend, no daughter. I had nothing. But I sat at the first table read, looking around the room, in awe. **That's Brad Pitt. That's Sir Anthony Hopkins. That's Marcia Gay Harden. How did I get here?**

Every day after shooting, I would return to my beautiful, empty apartment on Central Park West. I'd have something to eat, and then I'd go for a walk. But it wasn't just a walk; there was something pulling me out of that space. It was late spring, beautiful weather, and every night, I'd go walking around the Upper West Side. Usually, I'd end up in the Barnes & Noble on Broadway or a bar opposite Lincoln Center. About three weeks into this nightly compulsion to roam, I walked up to Symphony Space on Broadway at Ninety-Fifth Street where there was an all-night reading of James Joyce's **Ulysses,** an annual tradition held every June 16, a.k.a. Bloomsday. (If you've never read the book, the action takes place on June 16 and the hero is named Leo Bloom.) Every half hour, another actor would step in to read. I stayed for a couple of hours before that urge came back. I was like Leo Bloom on his quest through Dublin as I headed back down Broadway a few blocks until I came upon a jazz club called Cleopatra's Needle (presumably named after the ancient Egyptian obelisk parked in Central Park behind the Metropolitan Museum).

I went in and took a seat at the bar. I ordered a scotch and listened to the band that was playing. The light in the bar is rose-colored, turning everything pink. Then out of the bathroom comes this creature. She is tall, with light hair, I can't tell if it is blond or strawberry, and a face of such radiance and beauty. **I'm going to marry her.**

The place was packed, except for an empty stool to my left. She sat down and we talked and talked and talked. Her name was Kasia. She had no idea who I was, which was great. I told her I was doing a film and invited her to come to the set where we were filming in Brooklyn. We even talked about our notions of the ideal marriage. I drew a picture of two houses with a walkway in between the second floors. I'd gotten the idea from Raymond Carver and his second wife, Tess Gallagher, the poet, who lived in different houses in Seattle. If they wanted to spend the night together, one or the other had to drive across the city to the other's house. I thought that was perfect. (I'm tough to live with.)

About two hours into this blissful evening, I discovered that she was dating the piano player, and I walked out. I was devastated.

A few days later, a production assistant came to me on set and said, "Tasha called."

"Who? I don't know a Tasha." I went back to my trailer. **Bing.** I stepped back out and found the PA. "Do you mean 'Kasia'?"

"The person said 'Tasha.'"

"Call her back and invite her to the set."

The next day, she showed up at the Armory in Park Slope, where we were filming. She had taken the subway from Manhattan and brought a paper bag lunch of juice and a little sandwich. It was the perfect Joycean prop. In acting we say there is a moment in an audition where you win the role. It's the same in love. That paper bag, that simple, gorgeous prop, clinched it. I fell hard.

"Come here," I said. I opened the door to where craft service was set up. Back then, when you were on an A-list film with people like Brad Pitt and Tony Hopkins, craft service was major. There were carving stations as far as the eye could see.

I asked if I could give her a ride back to Manhattan. We went to dinner at Fiorello's on Upper Broadway, and we talked into the night. We saw each other every day after that. We ditched the piano player. We fell in love. Imagine Woody Allen's **Manhattan** or **Annie Hall,** those love letters to the city and to love itself, with "Rhapsody in Blue" the theme music. That's what our romance was like. New York was built for such love.

That walk I was compelled to take every night had led me straight to her, just as the walk to the San Francisco State College had led me to the theater. Those walks saved my life.

When I was done shooting **Meet Joe Black,** I went back to Los Angeles to resume **Larry Sanders** and my teaching at the Playhouse. Kasia joined me in L.A. I asked her to marry me, and she said yes.

And then things started to go wrong. Milton didn't like Kasia. He was jealous. He wouldn't invite her to the regular Friday dinners. He was rude to her. "She's not for you," he said.

"You're crossing a line that very few people can negotiate," I said.

Then, at a teachers meeting at the Playhouse, Milton asked me to sit beside him. He announced me as his successor, or words to that effect. He was giving me the Playhouse.

One Saturday at the master class, I was sitting in the theater with all of these other working, successful actors, waiting for Milton to arrive. When he walked in, Allen Garfield, a well-known actor who had been in **The Cotton Club,** stood and clapped. The rest of the class stood and clapped. One actor gathered his things and left, saying, "I'm outta here." I began to see it too. The thrall.

One Sunday, Milton called to summon me.

As I started to leave, Kasia said, "It's Sunday."

"But I have to go see Milton."

"It's Sunday. You have to choose."

Many years earlier, at one of the Friday night dinners, Milton had leaned over to me and said, "If I were you, I would run." I think he knew the best and worst of himself, and he was telling me, warning me, that he could be dangerous for me. He was a brilliant teacher, his critiques were genius, but as he once said, "It depends who answers the phone: Mephistopheles or the other one."

It finally hit me. I called him. "I can't do this anymore," I said.

I will never forget his answer. "Do what, sir?" He never talked like that. It was as though I had stepped into a Shakespearean scene. I was Prince Hal to his Falstaff.

"I'm out," I said, and hung up the phone. I never talked to him again.

Then Kasia and I went to breakfast. I was free. At that breakfast, Kasia insisted I call my daughter and mend that fence. "You're her father. She's your daughter. Pick up the phone."

I always felt guilty about leaving Milton so abruptly. People tried to get us to negotiate a truce, but he died without our ever speaking again. I was a pariah at the Playhouse. I still had two acting classes I was teaching, but I had to leave. I had to stop being a good boy. I had to get out from under the thrall.

## 16

## Fuck 'Em

Theater legend has it that when the late great Richard Burton was doing **Hamlet** on Broadway, he would stand by the curtain peering through a peephole at the audience and muttering, "Piss off." "Cunt." "Twat." "Wanker."

"Shite." As the cast was taking their places, they couldn't help but notice.

Finally, an acolyte approached him one day and said, "Sir Richard, what are you doing?"

Sir Richard said, "I'm preparing."

Here's what I think. I believe he was trying to remove himself from the audience's thrall—to be consumed by the need to please, the need for people to like you, to like your work. It is like being under a spell. That's certainly what it felt like at the beginning of my acting career.

I was always asking myself, second-guessing myself: **Is this the right posture? Is this the right line reading? The right costume? The right prop? The right timing? The right entrance? The right exit? The right . . . the right . . . the r . . .**

The crazy part is, the audience doesn't know you're in their thrall. You're in thrall to no one and nothing, to something that doesn't even exist. And that thrall is the death of spontaneity and invention.

This was Sir Richard's preparation behind the curtain every night. He was removing the spell. He was eliminating any sense of subservience to the audience so that he could be absolutely free in his decisions and choices in playing Hamlet.

I think this ability is not just a necessity, but it is one of the keys to the kingdom. To be clear, dear reader, the phrase is "fuck 'em." It's not "fuck them." It's not "fuck you"—especially not "fuck you," never "fuck you." It's "fuck 'em." It really should be written **fuckem,** actually. It's an attitude—not of hatred or aggression—but of freedom from self-censorship and the need to please.

When I was a student at San Francisco State, I loved jazz, and the city was a great place to hear it, especially the Jazz Workshop. All the big acts played there. One night the actress Connie Campbell and I went to North Beach like jazz pilgrims on the way to a shrine to see the king, Mr. Miles Davis. During the performance, whenever he did a solo, he turned his back to the audience. When the solo was over, he left the stage until his next solo. He was brilliant, and this was his way of making the audience listen. He was removing us so he could concentrate on his music. (On a side note, Miles Davis was one of the most handsome men I have ever encountered. Breathtakingly beautiful.)

Van Morrison, whom I adore, is also not warm and fuzzy in concert. He doesn't do patter between songs, and his whole demeanor comes across as less than thrilled to be there. He doesn't give a fuck that it's New Year's Eve and you spent a load to be in Vegas to hear his ass. He's just there to do his thing, throw down, and he kills.

There was a Greek restaurant in Los Angeles— fabulous food and a great atmosphere. An evening there would invariably end with waiters and clientele dancing around the tables outside, to the street and back. The first time I went, I didn't just make a reservation, I went to the restaurant in person.

When I arrived that evening with my mother and my daughter, we got the whammy—they stuck us in a cramped corner in the very back by the door to the kitchen. The next time I went, I didn't make a reservation ahead of time.

"May I help you?" the maître d' said.

"Yes," I said. "I would like the worst table you have and I would like to wait as inordinately long as possible."

There was a pause, and then the barest hint of a smile from the maître d'. "Right this way, Mr. Tambor."

After that, the maître d' and I became friendly, and he was a tough monkey, as Ernest Borgnine said to Frank Sinatra in **From Here to Eternity**. And he reveled in it. But he was a master, a real pro at what he did. He handled that restaurant like an impresario.

One day, I took him aside and told him how gloriously I thought he managed the restaurant. He didn't say, "Thank you." He didn't say, "You're too kind." He said, "Fuck 'em."

There's a scene in **The Hustler** after Paul Newman's character, Eddie, has lost his girlfriend to suicide, he's out of money, and he's got nothing left to lose. As he's racking the balls on the pool table, he turns to Jackie Gleason as Minnesota Fats, and he says, "You know, I gotta hunch, fat man. I gotta hunch it's me from here on in . . . I mean, that ever happen to you? When all of a sudden you feel like you can't miss?" That's "fuck 'em." It's a must in the rehearsal room; it's part and parcel of the actor's technique.

During the Summer Olympics in Rio in 2016, twenty-one-year-old Canadian swimmer Santo Condorelli had a unique pre-race ritual: he held up his middle finger toward his father in the stands, and the dad, from his seat, flipped one right back. His father explained that he'd started telling his son to flip the bird whenever he got frustrated—starting when the boy was the tender age of eight. It was a way to give himself confidence and tell the world "fuck 'em," so that he could get on with the race.

It's not that you don't give a shit—you do give a shit. It's not that you're relaxed; it has nothing to do with relaxed. I got a call from a friend I was in repertory with. He told me he had finally achieved a state of pure relaxation, and would I come check him out in the show he was doing? I did. What he had achieved was boring and flat. "Fuck 'em" is not that.

It's **not** being unafraid; who's not afraid? It won't slow your heart rate down; in fact, it will increase it because "fuck 'em" brings more tasks and makes you use even more of the colors on the palette. It won't make you happy; who's happy? I'm the Jewish son of Russian Hungarian parents—it's not even an option.

But it **will** make you more effective when you put down the heavy luggage being a good boy or girl; that's when your talent will come through.

It's this:

It's Picasso as an old man posing shirtless for a photo, proud as hell of who he is and what he's done, and in his world he's the handsomest man around.

It's an attitude. It is confident.

It applies even in the quotidian routines of everyday life. A friend of mine used to begin his day by saying, "I'm going to work to get fired today." That was his version of muttering through the peephole. He assumed an attitude that said, "Fuck it. Fire me if you don't like it." It freed him to do his work unfettered by fear.

I was recently called in to do a Sabra hummus commercial. Before you scoff, let me assure you that doing commercials and voiceovers is not to be sneezed at. Also, my family and I are huge hummus aficionados.

First of all, when you do voiceovers, you can wear shorts. (I'll pause while you picture me in shorts.) Second of all, it's really fun work, and you are paid thousands and thousands of dollars, enough to support the most alternative or revolutionary life you can imagine for yourself. (Also, I have four young kids and there is still college yet to come—do I make myself clear?)

Anyway, I was at the recording studio in Manhattan to do the voiceover for the hummus commercial. I was with a collection of people from the Sabra company and the ad agency, and we're sitting around waiting. Apparently someone was late, and we couldn't begin until this person arrived.

I decided to go out into the hall with my cup of coffee and read on my Kindle to pass the time. While I was out there, I saw this man coming off the elevator and heading in my direction. He was very Zegna'd and coifed and becuffed. He did not seem the sunniest of people. Ah, this must be the big boss we've been waiting for, I thought. As he passed me heading for the studio, I said to him, "Uh-oh. You're in trouble."

He stopped and glanced at me. He didn't smile or react in any way. He wasn't giving anything away. He walked into the room.

I stayed in the hallway a little longer, just a few moments more than I should. Then I entered the room and we began the recording session.

The big boss gave me nothing. I wasn't Jeffrey Tambor, I was just talent. But because of our initial meeting in the hallway, something, some chemistry, some relationship, some code had changed. Atoms realigned in a parsec.

Then this happened: About fifteen minutes into the session, I suggested a change in the script. "Excuse me, but I think it would be better if it went like this," I said.

Big pause. Everybody turned to look at the big boss. Apparently, no one talked to the big boss like this.

But then he nodded yes. His expression never changed.

And it was all because of the slight "fuck 'em" greeting in the corridor. It changed the room. He listened to me, and we had a great session. But that's not all. After I left that day, the boss apparently said some nice things and I believe it paved the way for me to do a very lucrative two-part commercial—that, and a huge amount of hummus was sent to our house.

The only way you can get a "fuck 'em" attitude, however, is to have spent time on the other side of it, in thrall, worrying: **Do they like me? Do they love me? Do they respect me?** Or, as my mother said every time I came from any event, whether it was a basketball game, Boy Scouts, or a school party, "Did they like you?" It is a hell to be avoided at all costs. This "Do you like me?," this "good boy," almost drove me out of the business.

When I was on **Max Headroom,** I was always trying to please others. It got so bad that I found myself in thrall to a guy from craft service. He was a total shit, doled out chili con carne like they doled out soup at a prison cafeteria. He always had this judgmental look on his face, and I found myself glancing over at him after each take, hoping to get one of his passive-aggressive thumbs-up. Him, of all people. But that's the thrall, baby, that's how it works its spell: it picks the schmuck, then you end up trying to please him.

Finally, I got so sick of being in thrall, I got to "fuck 'em." "Fuck 'em" says, "I don't care if you like me, here I am. This is all of me. I'm going to give you everything, because I don't care what you think. This is how it goes."

When I first did commercials, I used to walk in and pick out the person who voted against me. There would be eighteen smiling faces and one asshole frowning, the one who had said, "I don't like that guy." I would pick that guy out and I would ruin my whole day trying to get that son of a bitch to like me. Guess what? It never worked. It wasn't me, it was him. That guy was already broken; there was nothing I could do to change it. So fuck 'em. Rule of life: you do not want to go to the dance with the girl who doesn't like you; take someone else.

I've seen it in the acting classes I teach, when a student stops trying to please me, stops trying to "act" or to get a good critique, and just does the scene. It's always hands-down the most brilliant scene that student has ever done.

A lot of actors go into an audition to find out if the people on the other side of the desk think that they're talented. That's not how you get a role.

This is how you get a role. You walk into an audition with this attitude: "If you were to pay me, this is how I would do this role. If you agree with that, hire me. If you don't agree with that, adjust my performance. If you don't agree with **that** . . . then let's part ways as professionals and move gently on with our lives." It's called an audition, a word that literally means a "hearing," not a do-you-like-me or a do-you-think-I'm-talented or a do-you-think-I-have-a-future-in-show-business.

When I auditioned for the role of Jinx in **Mr. Mom** with Michael Keaton, I was asked to do a car scene. I walked in and sat down, and someone started to explain, "This is a car, so do the scene like you're driving a car."

I said, "You guys, I can drive a car, okay? So I'm just going to sit over here on this nice couch and do the scene." I got the role on that sentence. But I did a good audition, and I could tell by the looks they exchanged that I was hired. When I got home, I received a phone call telling me so. (This was before cell phones; I'll pause while that motherfucker soaks in.) My attitude showed them that I had confidence, a word I take very seriously. **Con** = with; **fidence** = loyalty to oneself. Loyalty to oneself. Fuck'em. And confidence spreads in the room: if the actor is confident, the director is more confident as is the producer and, oh boy, the casting director, and maybe, just maybe, the guy doling out chili on the set.

While I was doing **Sly Fox** at the Shubert Theatre in Los Angeles, I took a small part playing a designer on a television show called **Starsky and Hutch**. I believe the character's name was Randy. It was an okay part and I was going to be paid something like $500.

When I got to the set, I asked someone where the rehearsal room was.

"There is no rehearsal. You just do."

Someone else handed me the new pages—the part had changed in rewrites from the script I had been sent. Randy was now a flamboyant gay stereotype. It was toxic and harmful garbage.

I told the producer and director, "No."

They said, "What do you mean, no? You can't say no."

I said, "No. I'm leaving. Good-bye."

They said, "Just wait here. You can't go."

So I waited.

First, the head of NBC casting, Joel Thurm, called me. "You can't do this."

I said, "I'm doing this."

Then my agent called me. "You can't do this."

I said, "I'm doing this."

Someone from the network called. "Okay, okay, what do you want?"

"Make this character a person, a human being, not this awful, hurtful stereotype, or I go." I was able to all but dictate the script. Me. The lowest rung on the ladder.

To be clear, it was not that I put them back on their ethics, it was that I was costing them potentially a shitload of money. That's why they relented.

But from my perspective, it was the power of "No." It was fuck 'em. Some might say it was arrogance.

Sometimes the attitude comes from a place of ex-tremis, when you're so broken by something that you have no fucks left to give. The day my mother died, I got a call to pitch a series to ABC. I had partners but I was going to play the lead. One of my partners said, "Should we cancel?" I said, "No, let's do this." So I met them in the office of the high priest of ABC for this high-pressure pitch meeting. My partners started to do their spiel, and I could see they were being timid and it was not selling. I thought, **Fuck it, my mom just died.** I just didn't feel like being cowed and afraid that morning— so I grabbed the script and read a long paragraph, acting it with everything I had. Their mouths were hanging open. By the time my partners and I got down to the lobby, we got the call: the network bought it. They bought my confidence more than even the concept.

It's not just me. I had a student in one of my act-ing classes who had been struggling for weeks. Then one night she came in and did an amazing scene. "What happened?" I asked her. "What's different?" Her father had died the day before. I told her, "You should always act like your father has just died." It was electrifying.

However, there was at least one moment when "fuck 'em" backfired on me.

I always wanted to be in a Coen brothers movie. I so appreciate them, from their first endeavors to their last. They are truly outliers and wonderful artists. I was thrilled when I got an audition for one of their films, **A Serious Man.**

On the day of my audition, I drove to Sony Pictures. I stopped at the gate and told the guard, "I have a drive-on," which means I had a pass to drive onto the property and right up to the office where the audition was. The guard said I did not have a drive-on and directed me to the parking structure, which was about a mile from the office. I thought, **If I have to walk a mile to get to this audition, I'm not going to get the part.** It was too subservient. So fuck 'em.

"Okay," I said to the guard and waited until he averted his eyes, then I drove around the barrier and all the way up to the office. There was an empty space right in front, but there was one of those orange cones in it. I got out of my car, moved the cone, and parked. I was a little early, and I went inside to wait.

The casting director arrived first. She gave me a strange look and sat down. Then the Coen brothers came in. We were ready to start.

I had been asked to prepare for two different roles: a rabbi and a lawyer. One of the brothers asked me, "Which role do you want to read first?" The casting director was sitting behind them with a look on her face like she was working out a math problem.

I looked at the brothers, then down at my script. I made a decision right then. To this day, I don't know why I said what I said. "I think I'm going to read the rabbi. With the lawyer, you can do better." What I meant was, I don't like the part of the lawyer, and you can do better.

The room stopped, as though someone had poured Jell-O into it. The brothers looked at each other. I could tell this was a virgin moment for them. No actor had ever said anything like that to them.

As for the casting director, at that moment she put two and two together and thought, **Yeah, that's the asshole in my parking space.** She threw up her arms like a mafia chieftain as though to say, **Oh my God, what have you done?** See, casting directors get the flak when an audition doesn't go well, and I had just shit the audition bed.

I didn't get the role of the rabbi. That went to Alan Mandell. And the lawyer? I was right that they could do better than cast me, and they did. They cast Adam Arkin and he was wonderful, so much better than I could have done it.

And I'm pretty sure the casting director clocked me getting into my car in her parking space and leaving.

For all of you who may be thinking about adopting the Jeffrey Tambor fuck 'em philosophy, remember that this is part of it. If you're going to play the game, you have to play it no matter what. It's an attitude, a way of leading your life, not being hostage to fear of the audience or the boss or anybody else, just having confidence in yourself. Even if it means never getting another audition for a Coen brothers movie, which I didn't and probably never will unless one or both is reading this sentence—Hi, Joel! Hi, Ethan!—but even then it's a stretch.

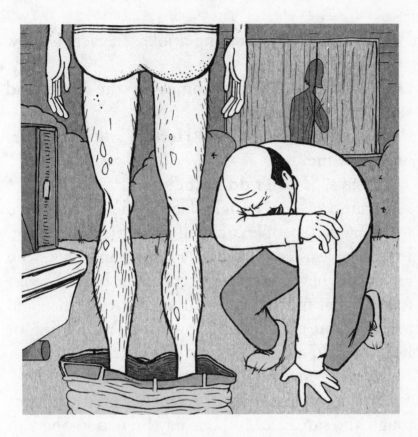

## 17

## Make 'Em Laugh, Make <u>Her</u> Laugh

**You can't laugh and be afraid at the same time.**

—STEPHEN COLBERT

I am incapable of telling a joke. In fact, I know only one:

**Old Mr. Cohen comes in the door and says, "Honey, I'm home."**

**Old Mrs. Cohen says, "Herbie, come upstairs and fuck me."**

**He says, "I can't do both."**

Because of my straight face, which I inherited from my dad, people can't tell if I'm kidding or not. I think he learned it from his Hungarian father, who reportedly never laughed, or joked, or indeed spoke to my father much at all. Harvey Fierstein once said to me, "**You** don't even know if you're kidding or not." He had a point.

For me, being funny was a deliberate decision.

I had a Spanish teacher in high school who was tough and sarcastic, and one day I'd had it. She said something snarky, and I said, "Oh, teacher made a funny!" I had no idea that I was going to say that and I don't think it was vintage Noël Coward material, but it got a laugh in the class. And the teacher's face told everything—she had been disarmed. I saw her immediately recalibrate our relationship. Humor is a negotiating tool with bullies. This is a bit too simple, but light is shed in the laugh, whether it be George Bernard Shaw or Beppy struggling for just a little respect in a Spanish class at Lincoln High School in San Francisco.

One night in November 2016, my wife and I attended a Broadway performance of **Oh, Hello.** The previous Tuesday, our house had been decimated by the presidential election news and now a very gloomy twosome was sitting in traffic on the way to Manhattan's Lyceum Theatre, listening to back-to-back depressing NPR news hours—transition teams in the Oval Office, rallies across the United States.

My wife, Kasia, said as we took our seats in the packed theater, "I've never needed to laugh as much as tonight." And we were rewarded. The two stars, Nick Kroll and John Mulaney, hit the stage running and broke every comic boundary in the book. They were fearless, irreverent, and heroic, and the laughs were earned. But that night there was a difference—there was a heart and a warmth and a need underneath the laughs. There was hunger for the sanity and health that is implicit in comedy.

It made me think of a night in 1963—November 23, to be exact. It was a Saturday, the day after John F. Kennedy was assassinated. I told Mom and Dad I was going to the movies. They were still staring at the television set like the rest of the nation when I headed out to a movie house on Nineteenth Avenue, which was showing the Steve McQueen movie **The Great Escape.** I thought I would be sitting alone in a darkened theater, but it was packed, every seat taken. As the movie started, Mr. McQueen made a simple sarcastic retort to one of his fellow prisoners (it takes place in a German prison camp during World War II) and it got what we call a "house laugh"—it was earned but it was also needed.

It was the same at **Oh, Hello.** I heard Kasia tell one of the actors as she hugged him in congratulations, "Oh, we so needed to laugh tonight."

Laughter is Darwinian, it is for survival, it is for health. There was a shaft of light in the Lyceum Theatre that night. Walking to our car on the chilly Manhattan streets after the show, we stopped at a halal stand to buy a lamb and chicken shawarma on pita with a fantastic yogurt sauce—twelve dollars, best meal in town. We were renewed with a sense of courage.

Humor has been an actual lifesaver for me. Growing up, I got pretty good at timing when my mother was about to go off and "zing" me with some less than complimentary comment. A favorite refrain of hers was "Look how you look."

Then one day, it hit me: If I could make my Spanish teacher laugh, maybe I could make Mom laugh and distract her from the onslaught, or at least buy me some time to figure out how the fuck to proceed. Yes, my humor is totally fear-based. When my antennae pick up danger and the Klaxons are going off, I get funnier.

The night they pulled me out of my acting class to come quick, my mother was failing rapidly, we drove up to the valet stand at Century City Medical Center and I asked the parking attendant, "If my mother dies, do I get free parking?" My assistant almost fell out of the car with embarrassment. Fear-based.

To my mind, Donald O'Connor's performance of "Make 'Em Laugh" in **Singin' in the Rain** is hands down the great song and dance number in the history of film. He dances around making an artful fool of himself, mugging and goofing and throwing himself through a wall with great precision, all in the service of laughter. Back in the audiovisual room at San Francisco State, watching him do that number over and over again, I would lip-sync along with the lyrics. It was my dirty little secret in the hip avant-garde theater department where we talked only of Ionesco, Artaud, and Camus. But the truth for me was the line "My dad said, 'Be an actor, my son, but be a comical one.'" Mr. O'Connor also breaks every rule in the comedy book.

One of the two (gulp) times I guest-starred on

**The Love Boat**—$5,000 and all the ignominy you can handle—I walked into a room on the set and there was an older woman who looked familiar. I wasn't sure if it was who I thought it was. I decided to ask the assistant director.

"Excuse me," I said, tapping him on the shoulder.

"Yes, Mr. Tabor?" (A common occurrence in those days.)

"Who is that woman sitting over there?"

He looked down at his clipboard. "Gish . . . Lillian."

D. W. Griffith invented the close-up for her and her sister "Gish, Dorothy" in **Orphans of the Storm.** I thought, **It's bad enough I'm here. Why in God's name is** she **here?**

She was sitting ramrod straight and looking at the lights being set and focused for her scene. If anyone knew light, it would be Lillian Gish. I asked her manager if I could talk to her.

"Oh thank you, would you? No one here knows who she is."

I sat in the director's chair next to hers, and I told her, "Thank you," and that we all stand on her shoulders. She smiled while continuing to stare straight ahead. Beppy Tabor knows how to pay a compliment.

On another part of the set, I saw my hero, Donald O'Connor, sitting next to a seal. Sylvia the Seal, or, to make that morning all of a piece—"Seal, Sylvia." She got billing ahead of me in the credits for the show, and she stank to high heaven. I thanked Mr. O'Connor for "Make 'Em Laugh" and confessed my San Francisco State vigils and how important that song was to me. "That song is why I'm standing here today." He said nothing. Also mute was Sylvia.

I've always thought comedy was serious business. If you go backstage at a comedy, you are likely to encounter silence. If you ask me, Aristophanes should have taken higher billing in the Greek theater than Aeschylus—very few of us fuck our mothers (**Oedipus**), while governments have young and old marching to war at a moment's notice (**Lysistrata**).

Anton Chekhov called his plays comedies because he was focused on man's folly. "To Moscow, to Moscow" in his **Three Sisters** was a symbol of our fallibility, the human ability to reach for the stars and end up staying home to watch the Food Channel. Jill Soloway's **Transparent** is a comedy in the same vein, because the Pfeffermans are simply and wonderfully human and ridiculous in their respective quests for freedom and authenticity.

I used to go with Jeff Altman to the Laugh Factory in Los Angeles to watch him do stand-up. I wanted to make a documentary that showed the journey from writing a joke to trying it out to standing it up. We waited at the bar while one comic after another tried out their material. The waiting performers were not happy or smiley. They looked as if this were an operating theater and complicated surgery was being done.

The most formative lesson I learned about humor was given to me by Barney Tambor, which is ironic considering my dad never went toward humor. He seldom smiled. As a Hungarian Jew, it just wasn't part of his deal. I noticed this trait when I visited Hungary. These are not a tap-dancing people. They still have bullet holes in the walls from World War II, which **ended more than seventy years ago.** But those holes say, "You see what can happen?"

So when the doctor came to his hospital room at the John Muir Medical Center in Walnut Creek, California, and told him it was time to go home, there was nothing more they could do for him, my dad looked at me and shrugged. **"Nu?"** (So?) I helped him dress and get packed up, including the marijuana to help with the side effects of the chemo. I rolled him in his wheelchair past the nurses' station. (His favorite nurse raised her hand and said, "Bye, Barney." A lesson in economy that broke one's heart to pieces.)

As we pulled into the driveway of their house, I saw my mother peering through the front curtains. She'd hardly ever visited him during his many stays in the hospital after his diagnosis, her fear of death was so great then. I parked and got out of the car. I walked around to the passenger side to help my father. He had lost so much weight in the hospital, as he stood up his pants fell to his ankles. I saw the drapes close.

And my father and I started to laugh . . . and laugh and laugh, harder and harder, banging on the roof of the car with our hands. Tears were streaming down our cheeks, tears of grief and hilarity all at once. Our inability to deal with the horrendous loss that was bearing down on us played out in belly laughs that could be heard up and down the street.

Not many days later, after the doctor's final visit to my father's bedside at home and that final shot of morphine, he was gone. At the funeral, a Reform rabbi in a rainbow yarmulke (thank God my dad was dead, because **that** would have killed him) who had never met my father starting singing a song on his guitar like one of the Kingston Trio; it went, "Barney, oh Barney," and my mother and I started to laugh. From behind, our shoulders heaving up and down, I'm sure people thought we were crying. It got so bad, I had to walk out of the synagogue and collapse outside in the Walnut Creek sun.

If there is a God, She lives within the sound of laughter. I search for humor like one of those old men with a metal detector on the beach looking for pennies. Laughter is the reason I'm living.

## 18

## No, No, No

Brian Grazer told me the best thing: "This is what a career sounds like: No, no, no, no, no, no, no, no, no, no, no, no, no, no, no, no, no, no, yes, no, no, no, no, no, no."

In my business, the business of show, two things

are certain. The first is that if you are an actor, you will be fired. I tell my students, "If you are any good, you will be fired." I must have made it sound good, because I regularly receive e-mails from students who tell me they can't wait to graduate and get fired. If you're ever stuck at a dinner party with actors and the conversation lags, just ask, "Have you ever been fired?" and you will be regaled with stories of dismissal for the rest of the evening.

The second certainty is that no one will actually say, "You're fired," no matter how that phrase has become part of our television-watching culture. Over the years, many other phrases have been used to sever relations. Sometimes, no words are used at all.

My friend Audra Lindley, the great screen actress and my costar on **The Ropers,** told me that she learned she was out as a series regular on a show when she drove onto the 20th Century Fox lot and found her parking space had been paved over.

I played a character called Murray for two seasons on the groundbreaking 1980s series **Max Headroom,** a dystopian satire in which television rules all (the Web was obviously not a thing yet). We were well into the second season when we began hearing grumblings that ABC execs were not doing headstands and slapping high fives when they saw the dailies. It was rumored the execs didn't even understand what the show was.

The premise was that an intrepid television news

reporter, played by Matt Frewer, is nearly killed when he uncovers a nefarious plot about lethal television ads, and his mind is copied into a computer, but the transfer doesn't go entirely smoothly, and the resulting Max Headroom character is a strangely stuttering, snarky version of the original. Although the Max Headroom character became a pop culture sensation far beyond the show, the execs didn't get it—even as Max Headroom's cartoonish face was emblazoned on the cover of **Newsweek** to kick off the season debut. What they **did** get was a reputed $2 million price tag per episode.

What the network not getting it meant for the actors in the cast was that we'd be in our makeup chairs in the morning having a coating of Max Factor #5 applied under our eyes, and the makeup artist would be saying, "Do you think it's going to be today?"

One Friday afternoon, Matt and I were shooting an argument scene in a warehouse in downtown Los Angeles. We were chewing some heavy scenery, as they say, when the doors to the soundstage burst open and sunlight flooded in. Our producer Brian Frankish ran in waving his arms. I could see the sweat stains in his armpits and his hair was thrown helter-skelter over his head.

"Ladies and gentleman! Cease your activity. Stop what you are doing immediately and walk away from your instruments now." Pause. "I said now! Walk away now!"

In what seemed like only a few seconds, all the crew and equipment vanished, and Matt and I were left, literally midsentence, alone in the empty warehouse. We looked at each other in stunned silence. Then, without a word spoken between us, we walked out to the street, down to the corner bar, and drank silently into the night. Somewhere around 11:15 p.m., Matt said a line only David Mamet would claim: "Oh fuck, we're fired."

My personal best in being let go happened on the next series I did after **The Ropers.** In 1982 I was hired by Jane Fonda to play the boss in the television adaptation of the hit film **9 to 5,** which is on the list of the American Film Institute's 100 Funniest Movies. The role of the sexist Franklin Hart had been beautifully played by the sensationally talented Dabney Coleman in the movie, and Dolly Parton's theme song was #1 on three **Billboard** charts and received four Grammy nominations and an Oscar nomination for best song.

I thought I was the hottest shit on the horizon when I got this gig. I was handpicked by Jane Fonda, who was producing the series for ABC TV. In our initial meeting on the Fox lot, she had called me—**me**—"Boss Man." Now my fame would go farther than far. I had a trailer next to my costars Rita Moreno and Valerie Curtin and Rachel Dennison on the 20th Century Fox lot. In short, I had arrived. And yet my then—let me repeat, then— agents felt compelled to tell me that the head of

ABC was not over the moon about my being cast;
he didn't want the bald guy, he wanted Dabney. I
guess my then agents were trying to keep me on my
insecure toes.

A week before we were to start shooting, Jane and
company were assembled for the first read-through.
Jane's role was as producer; she was the boss. In television, the read-through is all-important. If you were
looking for a carefree atmosphere, this was not the
place to find it. When I was first starting out, read-
throughs weren't so formal; they were kick-around
affairs for cast, directors, and writing staff with wall-
to-wall bagels and lox. Our table read for **9 to 5** was
jam-packed with studio and network executives, costuming, set direction, casting, production, and I believe one or two guys from valet parking. Yet with
all those people crammed into the one room, there
wasn't a sound. Everybody just looked at the head of
the table where the actors were supposed to sit at their
assigned places, complete with nameplates and scripts
with each actor's lines already highlighted in yellow
by a production assistant getting his or her first taste
of "show business." It looked more like a congressional
hearing than a table read, and it had about that much
warmth and humanity. The head of the network
walked around the table shaking the cast members'
hands. When he got to me, he didn't look me in the
eye; instead, he seemed to be looking at the middle
of my forehead, where my third eye would be.

Jane—yes, I was now calling her Jane—was

seated at the head of the table next to her producing partner, Bruce Gilbert. She stood and a hush fell over the room. She welcomed everyone, and talked about the show and what it meant to her and how proud she was of this endeavor we were about to embark on. And then she said the fateful words, "Have fun! There's no pressure!"

Oh, would that have been true.

We began the reading of the first episode. As sometimes happens during readings, there was a tendency toward over-the-top laughter, bordering on forced hysteria. I remember seeing people's faces dissolve into hearty guffawing, eyes filled with terror.

Normally, the cast would be excused at the end of the reading and the writers and producers would go into another room for notes or an "Oh fuck, here's the fate of our show" meeting. But Jane asked the cast to stick around while she and her producers stepped out. When they came back into the room about thirty minutes later, they looked confident and solid.

"Okay, any comments about the script?" Jane said.

Silence.

"Anything? Don't be afraid."

Silence.

"Hey, come on, guys. We're all in this together."

Silence. I couldn't say what I thought because I hated the reading, I hated my role, and I hated myself for taking the role. I hated my then agents for suggesting it. I hated my parking space and the cold coffee in front of me. I hated my chair, the table, and myself in television. I actually hated my television.

The character of the boss and Jeffrey Tambor were far, far apart. It wasn't even the character from the movie; it was a dumbed-down version for television audiences. The brush strokes were too broad, too farcical, too obvious. But I wasn't going to open my mouth because, hey, that was Jane Fonda sitting there. I knew I was riding a lame horse, and that lame horse was riding me.

The following morning, I shared my doubts about the quality of the script with my makeup man, who had trained with Benedict Arnold. By episode three, nobody on set, not crew, not cast, not catering, would look me in the eye. Conversation was limited to short, nonspecific sentences rather than any sort of meaningful exchange. I was being sent to Coventry, as the English say when someone is being ostracized.

I went home and told my wife, "I think something is wrong. No one is talking to me."

"You always say that," she said. "You're too sensitive. Enjoy the moment."

But I knew in my gut something was up. Every day, I'd catch a sidelong glance from a cast member, or the whispers of the director and writers. The absolute silence of my makeup man, Benedict.

I started to get so anxious that one morning I

woke up, went to the bathroom, looked in the mirror, and screamed, "What's happening?" like Dominique Dunne's character in **Poltergeist.** Staring back at me in my reflection was a HUGE-ASS PIMPLE in the middle of my face.

When I presented myself to Benedict hours later, he tried to cover it up with what seemed like a pound of Krazy Glue, which, rather than hide my defect, instead as good as announced to one and all, especially the cinematographer, "HEY, THIS FACE HAS THE BIGGEST-ASS PIMPLE YOU HAVE EVER SEEN IN YOUR FUCKING LIFE."

And the motherfucker wouldn't go away. For weeks, the cinematographer would have to grapple with shooting the other side of my face. And I would have to weather occasional comments from someone on the cast or crew: "Wow, that looks like it really hurts. Shouldn't you see someone?"

Things didn't improve.

In one episode, my character was having a meeting with a husband and wife, who were written and cast as Asian. I decided to do something one of my father's partners at Floorcraft, Jack Lerner, did when talking to Asian customers—talk to them in pidgin English. It didn't matter what level of education these customers had attained, PhDs from China were spoken to like infants. "You likey carpet? You makey big big money." So naturally, I decided to do that with my character. My character was a remarkable ass, remember.

The great Rita Moreno was in the scene with me, and after the first take she looked at me and said, "Oh Jeffrey, don't do this." I suspect she knew that things were not going extraordinarily well for me in the front office.

I proceeded.

The director laughed. The crew laughed. The cameraman laughed. Even the Asian actors laughed. But here's who didn't laugh: Jane Fonda, 20th Century Fox, and the head of ABC TV.

**CUT TO:** A month later, in my dressing room backstage at the Mark Taper Forum theater in Los Angeles, waiting to go on in the Georges Feydeau comedy **A Flea in Her Ear.** One of my fellow actors knocked on my door.

"Hey, Jeffrey, congrats on the show. I hear it got picked up. Way to go!"

I immediately went to the backstage telephone and dialed.

"Jane Fonda's office," the receptionist said.

"Hi. Jeffrey Tambor here." Pause. "Uh ... is Bruce Gilbert about? I'd like to talk to him."

"Hold on please." I'm treated to canned music for a long, long time until she comes back on the line. "Here's Bruce."

"Hi, Bruce. Jeffrey here. I'm down here at the Taper doing this play and I just heard about the pickup. I wanted to congratulate you. This is huge. I love it when the good guys win."

"Thanks," he said.

"Oh, uh, okay. Well, I'm around. Did the network give us a date when we're gonna start up again, because like I said, I'm around."

Silence. Silence. Silence. Then, "Uh, let me put you on hold for a second."

More music, a lot of music; it was a long, long second.

The stage manager comes up to me and mouths, "Five minutes to places."

Bruce finally comes back on the line. "Uh Jeff, we are—"

"Bruce, I gotta go. Is everything all right? What's up?"

"I'm sorry, we're going another way."

"Oh okay, I get you. What way?"

"We're going another way," he said again.

"Okay, Bruce, I gotta tell you, I've been giving this a lot of thought and I have some ideas about the character."

"We're going another way."

"Bruce, I get it. Another way. So is it my character or Valerie's? I have some ideas about Rita's, too."

"Hey Jeffrey? We're going another way."

"Is it my costuming? I think my color spectrum can be broadened, not so stereotyped."

Long pause.

"Jeffrey." I can hear Bruce take a deep breath, then exhale. "We're going another way."

Actors are moving past me, pointing to the stage. Props are coming and going, people are giving themselves last looks in the mirror.

Silence on the phone. Then it hits me. "So when you say you're going another way . . ."

"Yep," Bruce said. "Gotta go. Bye." Dial tone.

I gasped. **Oh fuck! I'm fired!** "We're going another way" is Hollywood for "Oh fuck, you're fired." **They're going another way, and it's without me.**

"Places! Places!" comes over the loudspeaker. "Ladies and gentlemen, beginners, please."

My fired ass and I proceed to make a frenzied and hysterical entrance to open a three-act Feydeau farce that would last the next two and a half hours.

Later, I asked my leading lady how I did, and she told me it was one of the most interesting performances she had ever witnessed. When I asked her why, she said that while I had delivered all my lines and hit all the choreographed moves that were called for, I never lifted my head once during the performance.

**CUT TO:** The Beverly Hilton Hotel, January 2015. The Golden Globe Awards. I had been nominated in the Best Actor in a Comedy Series category for playing Maura Pfefferman in **Transparent.** I and the vultures are sitting in my seat, very, very nervous. I'm good at some things, but award ceremonies and red carpet events are way beyond my abilities and leave me flustered. I can't eat, I can't drink, breathing is a challenge. The show has already won for best comedy, and the cast is poised to go backstage for photographs and interviews, but we're all waiting for my category to be announced. More awards, not mine. No one is talking to me or looking at me. And all the while, my story is playing in my head.

**ME: You're gonna lose this sucker. They have won and you are going to lose.**

The Russian-Hungarian tag team of my parents are having a rap battle behind my eyeballs.

BARNEY: **Don't celebrate, they'll take it away from you.**

EILEEN: **You're a piece of shit. You've always been a piece of shit. You'll always be a piece of shit.**

The cameraman comes over to our table and says, "Your category is up next," and proceeds to put the camera right in my face. A stage manager comes over and says if I win, I am to turn and walk this way, then this way, then left, then this way.

Back from commercial.

The presenters for Best Actor in a Comedy Series category are introduced: the stars of the new series **Grace and Frankie,** Lily Tomlin and . . . wait for it . . . Jane Fonda. When she walked out onstage, I knew I'd won. Why? Because God had made a circle for exactly this reason, and God, I have come to learn, is an ironist. They opened the envelope and announced my name.

I stood up, kissed the fourteen people at my table, and proceeded to walk to the stage, having completely forgotten the directions I'd just been given. I took every wrong turn, somehow ending up at the back of the stage. By the time I appeared, the applause had completely stopped. But there was Jane. The Bruce phone call evaporated. I looked into her gorgeous, shining eyes as she handed me the envelope. The circle was complete.

So the next time someone puts a troubled script in your hands and asks you what you think of it, I would advise you to open your fucking mouth, or you too will be told they are "going another way."

## 19

## Old Mrs. Cohen

There have been too many books already written on the subject of fear—and seminars, papers, lectures, TED talks. There is nothing I can really add. I am not an authority on fear. I am, however, an authority on **my fear,** and

I can wield a pretty good talk on that any time of the day.

I call my fear "Old Mrs. Cohen." She lives "in the back" and she is very, very cranky. She has no children, and old Mr. Cohen died of an aneurysm while watching **The Lawrence Welk Show** too many years ago.

Here's the deal—you know Mrs. Cohen is **there.** She has and will always be there. She has an original lease agreement with the landlord and is paying rent, but you never talk to her.

This very morning, I was watching a video sent to me by my friend Ben Barnes (he's the illustrator of this book and has been a friend for years) of Patti Smith (I love Patti Smith) in Sweden standing in for Bob Dylan at the Nobel Prize Award Ceremony.

There's a couple of things I already love going into this story.

First, Bob Dylan (love love love) got the award that normally goes to a book author or poet. I admire the grit of this choice. And if you watch the video, you can see there are those who are relaxed and grooving to the music and the message with their heads nodding to the beat. There are even those who are crying. And then there are those who look as if a tent pole has been inserted up their ass—and their necks have been cemented in rigor mortis . . . very uptight.

Two. When Bob Dylan got the phone call, he didn't get the phone call. Wherever they called, he didn't pick up. They couldn't find him. And this: Bob Dylan did not respond to the fact that he got the phone call for—wait for it—two weeks. That's not two hours, or even two days; that's Uncle Bob staying out of touch for two weeks. Some part of me— and I don't know if it's the healthiest part or the part that will get me into that special place in heaven— loves the fuck out of this.

Bob Dylan did not show. He said he would try, but he did not go to the award ceremony. He said he had—love love love—other commitments.

So Patti Smith—and I just watched it again— showed instead and sang "A Hard Rain's a-Gonna Fall." Not an easy song by any stretch, and you could tell the pressure was on. As the camera pans the audience, you can see who's in and who's out.

And then Ms. Smith goes "up"—loses the thread and fumbles—and tries to recover, then fumbles and stops and says, "I'm sorry." Voice quavering, a big pause. The orchestra stops. Everything onstage and, indeed, in Sweden stops.

She smiles as she apologizes. And that is key to this story—that is the source of this story, the smile, which recognizes us all as human and subject to error. It is the smile of acceptance of our fearful nature and what is at the core of our daily living.

And then she began again. It was no better or worse, it was her just back on track, but the audience **changed**. They were no longer viewers. They had in an instant become participants. If you look at the clip—and you should—you will see the change, you will see wife turn to husband and connect. You will see change in their faces. You will see human-ness. It is soooooo Bob Dylan, as if he were orchestrating by hand wires and marionette strings.

I live with Jeffrey fear every day. My particular brand has an interesting twist:

I'm afraid, or as Hugo Tambor says, "ascared," of the small stuff. It's not acting in front of a camera that arguably millions of people will see. It's: **Will the map that the transportation department has given me the night before get me there on time for tomorrow's shoot? So, maybe I should practice that drive tonight?**

How about making sure Evie is on time at school for her flute lesson? **Where did I put the flute? Did I leave it on top of the car? Oh my God, it's on top of the car and it's been there all night.**

My fear knows no discrimination. Each obstacle gives the same blast to my amygdala—**Ahooooga! Ahooooga! Dive! Dive! Will the coyotes get in the garbage again? Did I fasten that top correctly? Better check it again. Sure, it's four in the morning, but that's when your average coyote gets hungry, isn't it?**

I do know one thing about the amygdala—once that baby gets fired up, it takes about thirty to forty minutes to get back to "normal," and I use that word loosely.

Ready for a confession? I have a thing called the

"callback" and it has followed me pretty much all my life. I can date it to when it actually began, but it manifests itself this way. My friend Jill Clayburgh called me out on this. She said, "I always know you're going to call back and correct something you said or wonder if I was somehow offended by anything you said."

In days of old, when I would be interviewed, a reporter or journalist would sit with you, and during the back-and-forth notes would be taken. There was not a phone or an iPad to be seen. Nowadays, interviews are done in person with a phone stuck between you and said interviewer. A lot of the time, however, things are done **over** the phone, and said recorder is on the other end of the line.

After the interview, especially of late, when "things," as they say, are going rather well for Beppy Tambor, I will call the interviewer back and correct something I said, or make it clearer, or worry whether what I said was clear or needed more explanation.

It's this callback thing that is the matrix of "my fear." It is an act that is saying, "Are you there?" "Have I gone too far?" "Are you alive?"

My mother, having not succeeded the first time, tried to kill herself again a few years later, this time while I was away at graduate school. Again she fell short of the mark. I would phone her from Detroit. The phone sometimes would ring and ring and ring and my mind would race ahead to images of

stretchers carrying her out of the house to a waiting ambulance, my father attacking his face—
he would grab his face with his hands when he
became overwrought—the neighbors looking out
their windows: "There she goes again."

Or sometimes she would pick up: "Hello." In
that hello there was nothing. It was monotone and
disappointed.

"Hi."

**Hi . . .** even less energy than the **hello.**

"How's everything?"

"Oh, everything is just fine." (There has never
been a more sarcastic reading, nor more monotone.)

"Uh-huh."

"Did you call because you were worried?"

"No—no."

"Yes, you did."

And then I would start a sentence and she would
hang up midsentence. This was our ritual. I would
call back. Sometimes she would answer, sometimes
not. Our relationship had ground to this.

Every day, the threat that my mother would take
off for, if not greener pastures, at least pastures of a
sort. Now, when I talk to people and I worry if I've
been overmuch, I call back.

**Have I gone too far?**

**Have I been too much?**

**Will you be around tomorrow?**

In my acting class, I get confrontational and very
personal with my kids. I push 'em hard. Then I get

home and I wonder if I've pushed them over the edge. If I've been too much. I sometimes send an e-mail, checking—"Are you all right?"

**Beppy, your mother is very nervous.**

This is Beppy's fear. Checking. Always checking.

## 20

## Squeeze the Cans

I write the following not to hurt anyone's feelings or to denigrate any society, organization, or religion. When people ask me what kind of Jews my family were, I tell them that according to our neighbors in San Francisco, we were "dirty" Jews, so I am loath to come down on anyone's religious beliefs.

To find the path, sometimes you have to get lost. Back in the early 1990s, I got way, way lost while I was out looking for love, any love, all love, just love. My career was okay but not great. My first marriage had ended. I was treading water, trying to keep my head up until I got close enough to some shoreline I could grab on to. Around this time, I started dating a girl in New York. While I was waiting for her in her apartment one day, I found a paperback copy of L. Ron Hubbard's **Dianetics** on her bookshelf, with the fiery volcano on the cover and the preposterous number of copies that had been sold emblazoned at the top. I began reading. It was very good. It was very clear. I liked it.

Hubbard was a writer of more than a thousand books, mostly science fiction, who founded the Church of Scientology. He believed that pain and suffering were stored in units called "engrams" that were stored in the body and memory and could be reduced and eventually erased through a process called "auditing," during which the auditor would ask questions to the auditee, and by repetition the pain would lessen and disappear.

These units, or engrams, could be measured on a contraption called an E-Meter. The auditee would take a tin can into each hand and squeeze. The cans were attached to this meter and it would register the engrams visually. As I was reading that pain and suffering existed in physical units that could be broken down and gradually made to disappear like a calcium deposit, I thought, **Wouldn't it be wonderful if it were true?** I wanted it to be true. Apparently, I was not alone.

I kept flipping to the back page of the book to check and recheck the photograph of Mr. Hubbard, or L. Ron, as he was called. I was captivated by his wry smile, his hand cupped underneath his jaw. It reminded me of the smile of the man in Detroit who sold me my used Greenbrier station wagon knowing full well the backseat wouldn't fold down. Six hundred bucks, by the way. I didn't care, I loved that car. That car was my home for a decade as I crisscrossed the country having the best time of my acting life. I was totally willing to accept Scientology, even if it had a wonky backseat, if it would fix me. I needed fixing.

Of course, I was well aware of Scientology before this. I knew that my acting teacher Milton Katselas was a dyed-in-the-wool, hands-down, fuck-me-hard Scientologist. I admired Milton very much—as an artist, director, teacher. I wanted to know what he knew, what made him . . . him.

Sometime later, back in Los Angeles, I was dating an actress in Milton's class who was a Scientologist. She had already appeared in a couple of their training films. One day she asked if I would take a course with her. I think the class was called

2D Comm, which stood for "second dynamic communication," which is apparently what our relationship was, a second dynamic. I loved her, I loved Milton—I was game.

As I recall, the class was at the Celebrity Centre on the east side of Los Angeles. Hubbard had a thing for celebrities, which was smart because the biggest thing in Scientology is spreading the word, and what greater vehicle for spreading the word than a celebrity? That said, I was still a small fish at the time. **Larry Sanders** was still a year or two in the future, so the fact that I was deemed a celebrity the minute I walked into class, that was pretty heady for me.

The Celebrity Centre—that was how they spelled it—was a magnificent seven-story Norman Revival edifice that had once been a residential hotel for movie stars. That first night, we parked our car and walked through the gates, past the perfectly manicured gardens, and through a huge door to the study room. We were handed study packs and we took our seats. I began reading about communication. It was fascinating stuff. I loved it.

During the break, I was tapped on the shoulder by a man in a smart blue uniform. He beckoned me to follow him. I got up and walked down the long hallways, following him to an office deep within the building. At the far end of the room there was a desk, where a small lamp provided the only light.

On the wall was a portrait of L. Ron, again wearing that smile from his author photo and the ever-present ascot. A robust woman with red hair was sitting at the desk and a younger, slightly stocky brunette was sitting to her right. They asked me to sit with them. The room was almost womblike in its silence and protectiveness. No one spoke for the longest time, including me. They just smiled. Those smiles weren't smarmy, dear reader, they were sincere and I felt welcomed.

Finally, the woman behind the desk said, still smiling, "Why are you here? We had no idea of your interest."

"Nor did I," I said. "I'm just taking a course."

"We understand. Welcome."

"Thank you."

"We like Milton. A lot of his students attend here."

"Yes, I know."

Silence.

"We love your work."

"Oh, thank you."

The two lamp-lit figures were believers, and they loved me, Jeffrey, who had just come through the doors. I felt that love, I inhaled it. And I would for the next two years. I would take courses, and more courses. The first step remains my favorite. It was a class called the Student Hat. A "hat" refers to a job, as in you wear a particular hat when you do a particular job. I liked that; it seemed friendly and collegial. The class was all about how to study, which I enjoyed.

Hubbard's theory was that there were three obstacles to studying.

1. **Lack of mass.** If you're studying how a tractor works, you should have a tractor, or at least a picture of it, available.
2. **Too steep a gradient.** Make sure the gradient for learning is accessible. You can't learn a thing if you haven't fully learned the previous thing upon which it's based.
3. **Misunderstood words.** Hubbard maintained that a single misunderstood word could prevent a student's understanding of a subject. This part included sessions with the **OED** and Merriam-Webster. Are you kidding me? I was in heaven.

You never had to worry about your next course, because that was laid out for you. The whole process is called the "Bridge to Total Freedom," and you're supposed to go up it during your time there. You have your advisers, the ladies and gentlemen in the uniforms; it is part of their mission to make it **your** mission to move on spiritually and eventually "go Clear," a level of spiritual being out of reach of most Thetans. Oh, a "Thetan" is a spiritual unit—you and I are operating Thetans. I even liked the name. Hi, Thetans!

During my first year, I did what Hubbard called a detox, which had me sweating in a sauna—we Jews, for centuries, have called it a **schvitz**—and taking superhuman levels of niacin for months to rid myself of the poisons I had accumulated in my fat cells. What niacin also does when taken in thousands of milligrams is turn your ass bright red and scare the holy shit out of you when you look in the mirror of your locker as you undress to go into the sauna. It is also quite effective and is being adopted in many drug treatment programs now.

As a celebrity in Scientology, you are special, and you are treated, you guessed it, specially. The following is a list of seldoms you do as a celeb:

- You seldom have to go in a regular door of any building. You go in the back or, at the very least, the side.
- You seldom wait in a line—ever—for anything. If there is a line, you are not even made aware of it. You are lineless now.
- Where you walk is seldom peopled.
- You seldom go to a regular classroom. You go to a special classroom just for you, that has mahogany and teak as far as the eye can see, and comfy chairs to sit upon during your three hours of course study.

I liked the classes. I liked the auditing, squeezing the cans and recounting stories about my past lives. I seemed to have dwelled in Washington, DC, during Abraham Lincoln's tenure (I was reading Gore Vidal's **Lincoln** at the time).

I liked the **schvitz**. I liked the people who taught and worked and studied there. I liked that Scientology was outré and somewhat frowned upon; I liked the edginess of that.

It was all enough to turn a boy's head. I was happy. I bought in. I felt the love in the building and in the hearts of these people and I actually believed I was a Thetan who was going Clear. That's all I wanted. I wanted to go Clear and stop.

And that was the problem. They wanted me to go Clear and not stop—ever. They wanted me to keep moving up the Bridge through all the levels, which had fantastic names, but you had to pay to find out what those fantastic names were. I would have happily continued, but the courses were, shall we say, pricey.

I said, "No."

They said, "Yes."

I said, "No."

They said, "C'mon."

I said, "I have no cash."

They said, "This is why American Express was invented."

I said, "Maybe."

My business manager said, "You know, with Judaism you only have to kick in at the Rosh Hashanah gala once a year."

And then, one morning, I was awakened in my house in Van Nuys by the sound of fall leaves crunching outside my bedroom window. I rose to investigate, and outside in the morning fog were two figures moving stealthily about. In the gloom, I could just make out the glint of light on the brass buttons of their blue jackets.

**DING**

(fuck)

**DONG**

I opened the door to two smiling faces.

"It's Thursday, and we are here to sign you up today to make our weekly quota of points." They were a married couple, members of Sea Org, facilitators of Scientology who signed up for literally thousands of years of service. They couldn't have been nicer. Which is why I felt a little bad when I said, "No," and closed the door. I returned to my bed to stare at the ceiling in disbelief.

This was starting to get weird. There was a level of paranoia in the organization that was disconcerting. And the sycophancy was beyond the pale. There were busts of L. Ron every four feet in the Center—sorry, the Centre—and the standing ovations at some of the convocations were gratuitous, knee-buckling rounds of standing and sitting and standing and sitting every time L. Ron's name was mentioned. It was good for your core, I guess, but transparently unnecessary.

Strangely enough, shortly after my dawn visitation, I was asked to audition for the voice of L. Ron for various training films, and I agreed. Indeed, I was flattered. I found myself driving an hour and a half through the desert to Hemet, California, where Scientology HQ is located. I was led to a recording studio. I sat at my high stool in the studio with my scripts on a music stand in front of me and tested the mike.

"One, two, three. Testing. Testing. Jeffrey Tambor, testing for the voice of L. Ron Hubbard—"

And that's when it hit me. **What the fuck am I doing? Where the fuck am I?**

I thought of my dad saying when Larry and I were kids, "At the end of the day, you have your integrity. Remember, keep your nose clean."

I proceeded to "boot" the audition. I made his voice a little higher and just a tad whiny. And then very growly and orotund. I saw the heads turning toward one another in the control room. They asked for another take. I did it again, this time with just a slight basso tremolo—think, Boris Godunov meets **Dianetics.** I was very nervous about this obvious tanking, but I didn't want to be the voice of anybody other than myself, thank you very much.

Then there was the con man. Reed Slatkin was another dyed-in-the-wool fuck-me-hard Scientologist, from the time he was a teenager. He was also cofounder of EarthLink and ran a shady investment company out of his garage. He smiled constantly, his breath stank, and he got lots of people in Scientology to invest with him to the tune of nearly $600 million by promising to help church members "up the Bridge." At least, that's what he told my business manager when we met with him at my house. In a classic Ponzi scheme, he paid earlier investors with money he bilked from later investors, like me. He then cited the great "returns" the earlier investors received to con more of us to chip in. In the end, he conned me out of thousands of dollars, and he ended up serving about ten years of a fourteen-year sentence. Word was he funneled to Scientology a lot of the money he brought in, but the church disavowed him, so who knows?

So was that the final straw for Jeffrey? Nope.

I was called to what is called "Ethics" at the Org. I was seated across the desk from a young man in Sea Org uniform, minus the jacket, just white shirt and tie. His title was Senior Ethics Officer, although he looked like Opie in the **The Andy Griffith Show.** Hi, Ron. (I mean . . . the other Ron.)

And he had skin that looked like a polenta festival and anachronistically slicked-down hair. Unsmiling and businesslike, he began to tell me of the organization's worries about my progress moving up the Bridge since I had stopped showing up for classes.

"We think you are being influenced by an SP."

**The Southern Pacific Railroad?**

Then I got it—an SP is a suppressive person,

someone who is, according to Scientology, "actively working to suppress the well-being of others." An SP in your vicinity can make you yourself a PTS— Potential Trouble Source. "The suppressive person keeps the potential trouble source from functioning in life," which made no sense in this case because Kasia was the reason I **was** functioning in life.

"We think you should disconnect from her."

I thought Milton and the Playhouse had something to do with this little meet-and-greet. He wanted me to disconnect from Kasia too, and he had very close ties to the Celebrity Centre and was known for marshaling a number of his students to embark on the expensive journey up the Bridge.

There was a pause that would have made Harold Pinter stand up and take notice, and then I said, "Guess what line you just crossed."

"Sir?"

"I'm out."

"Sir?"

I stood up and walked out, slamming the door behind me. Just like with Milton and the Playhouse, I was never going back. (You guys can stop calling me now. I'm good.)

No hard feelings.

## 21

# Reading at the Greyhound Bus Terminal

G eorge C. Scott once said, "You know what I regret? I can't go watch people at the Greyhound Bus Terminal anymore."

It is a great lesson: Go down to the bus station, bring no book or smartphone, and just start reading what's in front of you. Remember it, store it. Milton Katselas, who actually directed George C., did the same thing. We would go to restaurants and watch people. We would make real-money bets on what people's occupations were, and then one of us would go over and politely inquire to find out which of us had won.

My first teacher at San Francisco State, Dale Mackley, had us keep an observation notebook with us everywhere we went. He told us it was the secret sauce of an actor's technique. In trying to live lives of integrity and meaning, we are often little more than a blooper reel of mistakes and embarrassments and overstatements and fulminations.

Ladies and gentlemen of the jury, I give you some of my favorites:

- Our neighbor across the street when we lived at 102nd Street and Broadway in Manhattan would come out every morning to put her trash in the bin, then look up at the sky and scream, "God damn it!" and then go back inside.
- I was having dinner with a friend at a posh eatery in Lower Manhattan. The waiter was uptight and curt with us all evening—I'd say, 30% passive, 70% aggressive. At the end of our meal, I asked for sherbet.
  "You mean sorbet?"
  "Sure, okay."

"We're out."

He then piled our dishes on his tray and abruptly walked away. A moment later, there was the sound of dishes crashing down the stairs to the kitchen, an explosion of sound straight out of a Feydeau farce. Like the Beatles said, "Instant Karma's gonna get you."

- Years ago I joined a USO tour to entertain our armed forces throughout eastern Asia and the western Pacific. We traveled from USO club to USO club in Japan, Korea, and Guam. We often dined in the officers' club after the show. One night we were sitting at a table with a high-ranking officer and his wife. The "talent" did all the talking, while the officer and his wife listened politely . . . and drank. At the end of the meal, as we were all standing up to leave, the officer's wife leaned down to get her purse and the officer whipped her around and without a word slapped her full-strength across the face. She picked up her purse and they left.

- I love diners. When I'm in New York City, I also seek them out. My favorite is the Metro on the Upper West Side. But before diners, my passion—and this dates me—was for automats. They used to be all over the city. For those of you under 100, an automat is a self-service joint. You want a sandwich? Open the glass case where the sandwiches are on display in separate compartments. Same for pie or my favorite rice pudding. You take your food and your cup of coffee over to the cash register and pay, then select a Formica-topped table to your liking. Mine was in the front corner facing out toward Fifty-Seventh Street.

One day I was seated and a man took the table next to me. He was nattily dressed in a plaid suit with a vest and bowtie. His hair was thin and blond. But here's the thing: his fingernails were long. Like, Mandarin long. He asked me what I did for a living, and I told him I was an actor starting out in New York.

"And what do you do?" I asked.

"I'm going to kill President Carter."

- The streets of New York are a great democracy. Titled and untitled walk the same crammed pavement. One day I was walking down the East Side when I stopped at a light. There were quite a few people jammed up against one another waiting for the light to change. I noticed the woman to my left. She was dressed all in black and wearing a black hat like a tall beret. But it was her neck and the absolute stillness of her face that drew my attention. She held her head high, her neck perfectly aligned with her body. She was looking left and right without moving her head, the way my basketball coach had taught us—so as not to give away your intention to your opponent.

I kept my gaze ahead as I whispered in her ear, "I won't embarrass you, but thank you for everything, Miss Garbo." Greta Garbo, arguably the biggest star of the 1940s, continued to look straight ahead. "Thank you," she said, with the slight hint of a smile on her lips. That regal neck had supported that face that had changed motion pictures forever.

- I have a fear of being fat. Let me clarify—I have a horror of being fat. My career is a display of differing weights and protruding bellies. I hit my limit while filming the movie **Pollock,** and I did a scene with Ed Harris in a DeSoto. I got in the car, and it **tipped.** The diet and the sobriety began, and I've been in relatively good shape and poundage for some years now.

All of this is preface to this:

I used to go to the trendy Ma Maison in Los Angeles. The chef was Wolfgang Puck and the clientele were the crème de la crème of Hollywood. There was Peter Falk at one table, John Cassavetes at another, superagent Sue Mengers over there. And then at one table was a man sitting by himself. He was enormous. He had to be in the heavy 300s, but this was what was so remarkable: His table manners were dainty and precise. He cut his meat with surgical skill and ate very slowly. Patience and exactitude, that's how you play "fleshy."

- My dad, Barney Tambor, the man who went to every play and every baseball game I was in, once came to see me backstage when I was doing **Sly Fox.** He murmured his congratulations, but he wouldn't smile, he wouldn't open his mouth. The reason? His front teeth were missing. During his flight, he'd tried to open the little package of peanuts with his teeth and the peanuts won.

  Here's another thing about my dad. When he ordered coffee at a restaurant, he would pour a little bit out into the saucer, blow on it, then pour it into another cup. He kept doing that until the coffee in the original cup had cooled enough to drink. If you brought that behavior to the set, you'd probably be met with an argument from the director. But Brando would have used it, I assure you.

- On the Amtrak train to Boston from Washington, DC, there was a man in a blue suit, his hair slicked back and parted on the side. His nails were manicured, and his shoes were shiny and new. There was a pin of some kind on his lapel. An American flag? A congressman, maybe? Here are the two details: 1) He cracked his knuckles one by one, over and over again. My brother used to crack his knuckles before he went to sleep. Just once through; I'd count the ten cracks of his ten fingers, then I'd fall asleep. This guy kept cracking and cracking and cracking, while his leg bounced up and down. 2) He spent the whole journey talking quietly, but I saw no cell phone or earpiece. He was talking to himself.

These are people and this is how they behave. Pay attention. God is in the details, as every good writer knows. People are not generalities or abstraction; they are a collection of specifics, detail upon detail upon detail. In observing those details, you will discover this axiom: People are ridiculous.

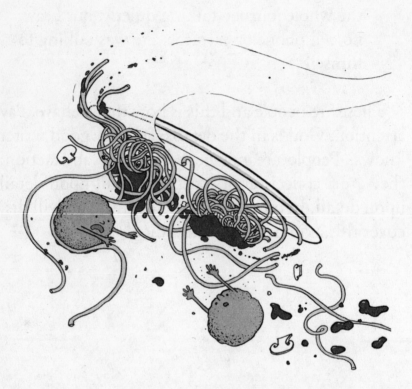

## 22

## Unhappy Hour

"**M**ake it a double. On the rocks. Hurt me."

That's what I used to say to the bartender.

When I got **The Ropers,** the confluence did me in. My brother, my hero, gone. My father, my protector, was going, soon to be gone. And . . . now, less than honorable work in television, work we scoffed at.

In Television City, I walked to the end of the building between rehearsals of **The Ropers.** It was the day **And Justice for All** came out. I stared out at the Los Angeles skyline. **How did I get here? This very building is where my dad took me as a kid. This is where I met Red Skelton, my boyhood hero. What have I done? This is not Broadway. What is this "Los Angeles"?** As Gertrude Stein said, "There is no there there."

Here—**$6,000 dollars per week. Ten times what I earned on Broadway working my tits off, exactly. I don't need $6,000 per week. I don't do anything.** City Slicker is where I drink at five—after rehearsal across the street from TV City. I have a charge account—Greg, my business manager, thinks I'm buying raincoats. "Why so many raincoats?" he says.

"Make it a double. Hurt me."

Go to my friend's apartment building on Sunset and Sweetzer, do laps for thirty minutes. Perhaps the best shape I'd ever been in.

Then drive back to the Slicker and sit with D. my director and C. the script girl. D. keeps looking at his watch. It's a TV director thing—always know what time it is and where you are.

Where am I? How did I get here? And drink and drink and laugh and smoke cigarette after cigarette.

I had a wife and child at home, and I was not there. What they had was: the spaghetti sauce stain on the dining room wall where I threw an entire serving dish, and the smashed glass of the double doors out to the swimming pool that I had thrown my glass against.

Danger was a huge ingredient, trying to get in as much trouble as possible, because in the absence of being creative it at least felt like being creative. Getting into trouble, finding the edge, immersing myself, losing myself. And trouble I did get.

I woke up in many strange beds—one time I woke to find a naked woman doing bicep crushes in front of her mirror. Had we had sex in a gym? I had no idea because—wait for it, again the irony of our Creator—blackout. I couldn't remember a fucking thing. There were buttons and lingerie on the floor. No idea what had happened. I would make my way home, the sun coming up as I sat by the side of my pool shaking, my wife inside getting Molly ready for school.

Brick in **Cat on a Hot Tin Roof** talks about the **click.** For me, it was the **ahhhhh.**

The pain in my chest, deep down, that ache, would cease for a time . . . until morning.

This memory: In a jazz bar one night, I had gone to the bathroom while the Don Randi band was on break. Coming back, I passed behind the trumpet player talking to the bartender. "That is the saddest person I have ever seen," he said.

He was talking about me.

It was Kasia who got me to help, to Dr. Ron, recommended by a friend. Kasia and I went together.

"Do you drink?"

"Yep, I do."

"Yes, he does—too much."

"Do you think you might be an alcoholic?"

I laughed out loud at the lunacy of this. "No."

And then **tick, tock**. The finger pointed outward . . .

**Eileen was an alcoholic.**

**Larry died of alcoholism.**

**My sister is MIA and was addicted to heroin.**

. . . and started moving slowly around back to me.

**Cleff is an alcoholic. He is heading for the Colma cemetery to rest right next to Larry and Grandma and Grandpa Tambor.**

I was ashamed of taking my brother's place, and being so, I actually took my brother's place. Dutifully, I became the drunkard. I bonded with my mother in booze. Now I bond with my mother in Maura. One of Maura's signal traits is the hand clasped around the neck. That was Eileen's.

As of February 15, 2017, I have been sober for fifteen years.

Thank you, Kasia.

Thanks, Mom.

Hi, Dr. Ron.

## 23

## Garry

Ne night in the late 1980s, after my run on **Max Headroom** had ended—**Step away from the instruments now!**—and I was, as they say, between engagements, I was watching TV (as we did back in my day), idly flipping channels, and then suddenly before me on the screen was this wonderful show called **It's Garry Shandling's Show,** one of the first originally scripted series to appear on the cable channel Showtime. I didn't know who Garry Shandling was at the time, but I was riveted by his innovative comedy. **He's looking straight into the camera—nobody looks straight into the camera. Who is this?**

He was breaking the fourth wall and he didn't care. He wasn't even breaking character to address the viewing audience; this **was** his character. It felt like he was talking directly to me: **Jeffrey, this is how it's supposed to be done.** The character "Garry" tells the audience he's got to go to the bathroom and the credits will run while he's gone. And then comes the silliest, most sublime theme song I have ever heard.

This is the theme to Garry's show,
The theme to Garry's show.
Garry called me up and asked if I would write
    his theme song.
I'm almost halfway finished,
How do you like it so far,
How do you like the theme to Garry's show.
This is the theme to Garry's show,
The opening theme to Garry's show.
This is the music that you hear as you watch the
    credits.
We're almost to the part of where I start to
    whistle.

Then we'll watch **It's Garry Shandling's Show.**
**[whistles]**
This was the theme to Garry Shandling's show.

I later heard that Garry and Alan Zweibel wrote the song during an elevator ride.

To me, his show went beyond comedy, because it was not only funny, it was clever, and it had something we don't ever have much of in our society anymore—wit. The lead character, played by Garry (obviously), was a standup comic who knew he was starring in a sitcom, and so did the other characters. And so did the studio audience.

There was Garry Shandling, a young man who seemed to trust the audience with his material, and it made you feel better as a person for watching it. It was more than that he broke the fourth wall and addressed the viewers during the show; it was that he seemed like a real person who was really talking to us. He went beyond the joke to another realm that not only invoked laughter but also revealed something real about people.

**It's Garry Shandling's Show** didn't have a laugh track. Instead, this show left the audience response up to the audience. You could laugh or not. You were being entrusted to respond to the show in any way you wanted. A smile, if you wanted, would do.

In 1992, I was called into a meeting with Alan Zweibel for a sitcom pilot for NBC. Alan had been a writer on **Saturday Night Live** and was now a producer. As soon as I sat down to read, I knew this show wasn't right for me. Alan and I looked at each other, and I saw that he knew it too.

He said, kindly, "You're very good."

"Thank you. I know I'm not right for this role."

"So what are you doing here?"

"I'm not all that sure," I said.

"Do you mind if I do something?" Alan said, with a curious look in his eye. "Do you mind if I make a call to a friend of mine?"

"Who is it?" I asked.

"Just a friend."

He got up from the desk and went into another office to make his call. A few minutes later, he came back into the room and said, "I just called my friend Garry Shandling, who's doing a show called **The Larry Sanders Show** for HBO. They're having a bit of a problem casting this role called Hank Kingsley. And I think you're Hank Kingsley, and I told him so."

That guy who talked to me from the TV and made me feel like an adult, **that** Garry Shandling? "Great!"

So the script came to my house, and it was called "Hey Now!" I had no idea what those two words would come to mean in my life.

But first, let me give you a little backstory on my friend Garry. During the early 1970s, well before he started his eponymous, revelatory sitcom, before he ever did standup comedy, Garry wrote for some of the top traditional sitcoms on television, like

**Sanford and Son** with the brilliant Redd Foxx and **Welcome Back, Kotter,** which spawned the mega career of John Travolta. In the '80s, Garry was a frequent standup comedy performer on Johnny Carson's **The Tonight Show.** So Garry had some serious chops in show business, and Johnny liked him so much that he eventually became a regular guest host on the show. A lot of people thought he might even replace Mr. Carson when he retired.

Instead, Garry came up with this idea for a kind of meta fake talk show, with real celebrities coming on for interviews, and all the insanity that went on backstage when the cameras weren't rolling (on the fake talk show—they were rolling on us, if you follow). The character of Hank Kingsley was sort of the Ed McMahon sidekick to Garry's Larry Sanders.

There are a half a dozen moments in an actor's career when one reads a script and thinks, **There it is.** Hank Kingsley was that role. There was just something about him that I really, really liked—no, not liked, **knew.** I knew Hank.

On the day of the audition, I had a three o'clock appointment. I left my house at maybe 11:00 a.m. for what was at most a forty-minute drive to the studio right opposite Paramount. I drove round and round, listening to music, making concentric circles, smaller and smaller, until at three o'clock I was at the studio. It was like a special ops assault.

I parked my car and went inside.

Garry was there with the great casting director

Francine Maisler. Garry didn't know who I was, only that Alan had recommended me. There was a camera set up to record the audition, during which I would be reading with Garry. The scene was Hank Kingsley explaining to Larry why he said, "Hey now!" which was driving Larry crazy. While we read, I noticed Garry looking over at Francine. I thought that was a good sign and plugged on.

Then there was a moment in the scene when Larry wanted to leave the office and I was to stop him with my voice, to yell "Hey!" or something like that. Instead, when Garry/Larry started to walk out, I picked up this long couch that was there and pushed it in front of the doorway to block his exit. Garry stopped, and he looked at Francine again.

It's my theory that you don't get a role by just reading a part well. There's a moment in a reading where you get a role, and you have to hit that moment. And what I did with that couch I think was that moment.

Garry turned to me and said, "Please go sit in the waiting room."

I left the office and took a seat in the waiting area outside the office. I knew my audition had gone really well. Penny Johnson Jerald was the next to go in to audition—for the role of Larry's assistant Beverly Barnes. We still argue about the timing, but I am sure this happened: While she was audition-ing, Garry would every once in a while yell out to me, "I haven't forgotten about you!"

The odd thing is that when Penny was through, they didn't call me back in. I was excused. But for some reason Garry had wanted me to sit there. (It was one of Garry's many idiosyncrasies, which I grew to like—no, love.)

A few hours later, around six or seven o'clock, I picked up the phone and I called Garry's office. It was completely out of character for me to do something like that.

"Is Garry Shandling there?"

"Who is this?" the voice said.

"It's Jeffrey Tambor."

"Please hold."

It turns out Garry was at the gym, but they put me through to him there. Garry came to the phone a little breathless and said, "Hi, how are ya? What's up?" I was kind of amazed he took the call.

"Garry, I have to play that role," I said. "I was born to play that role. For the record, I don't do things like this."

"Yes, but Hank does."

Well, that seemed promising. Still, Garry took his time to decide. Months passed. My agent would make up stories like, "Jeffrey has another series," or "Jeffrey has a movie offer"—I had nothing, let's be honest—but Garry wouldn't budge. He was meticulous about casting that show.

At one point he called me at home and said, "I'm watching **And Justice for All** right now."

I thought, **If he's watching that, then he really**

**does not know who I am.** But I knew I was getting close. (I found out only recently that Judd Apatow, who was a writer on **The Larry Sanders Show** then, had told Garry to watch it. Judd was a big fan and I frankly owe him a lot. He was in my corner all the way.) Hi, Judd. Thank you, Judd.

Finally, I got the call to read for the late, great Bernie Brillstein and Brad Grey, the co-heads of Brillstein-Grey Entertainment (which would later produce another groundbreaking show for HBO you might have heard of, called **The Sopranos**). I believe there were some executives from HBO there as well.

On the day, I was sitting there facing all of them. By way of introduction, Garry said something like, "I'm very excited about uh uh uh uh uh—"

And I said, "Jeffrey?"

It got a huge laugh. And I thought, **I'm in,** because that is the relationship between Larry and Hank.

Indeed, I got the role. My agent at Gersh, Leslie Siebert, said to me, "This is a game changer." And it was.

Shortly after I got the role, Garry invited me to go with him to a taping of **The Tonight Show** with Johnny Carson in which Garry would be the lead guest. When we got to the studio, he asked if I wanted to go backstage, but I declined. I wanted to give him his space and give myself space to watch and learn. I sat in the rear of the audience, and waited. The lights dimmed, and Ed McMahon came out to warm us up. The audience, me included, ate it up. While the audience laughed, I, with every mimetic bone in my body, tried to suck Ed up into my being.

Then Ed counted down to air: five, four, three, two, and then, "Heeeeeere's Johnny!"

I was surprised by one thing during Mr. Carson's monologue. On television, when Mr. Carson hit a joke, the camera would cut to Ed laughing, as though he were across the stage. But he was only about ten feet away. They were practically standing next to each other. Ed was right there supporting him. That was the what and why of his existence. I learned everything I needed to know about Hank Kingsley in that moment.

After the monologue, lesson number two happened. As they went to commercial, the lights dimmed, and Ed McMahon and Mr. Carson just turned in silence and took their respective seats far upstage. During the two-and-a-half-minute break, they didn't speak or interact in any way, the two men silhouetted against the backdrop of Los Angeles. I was enrapt. I later begged Garry to have Larry and Hank do this; I think we did it once for thirty seconds, but it was an indelible moment in the show.

Then Garry came to do the first of two segments. It was obvious how much affection Carson had for him. But I could tell that Garry's routine was a little off. At the commercial, the lights dimmed again, and I saw Garry reach into his suit pocket and pull out some index cards. He went through them and reshuffled the order, calmly and with the precision of a scientist. He knew what was happening and he changed it in the moment. When the lights came up and Garry resumed, the jokes started to hit and I could see the look on Carson's face: Garry killed. It wasn't the first time Garry would teach me a lesson about spontaneity. And to remember the cards can always be reshuffled.

The thing that I loved about doing **The Larry Sanders Show** was that not everyone got it at first. The writing was remarkable—Garry never went for the easy joke, he went past the joke to the character reveal. If you were a writer who got that, you excelled. The writer who went for the joke did not do as well. When the writing or the performing was going well, Garry would say, very simply—without laughing, but meaning it—"That's hysterical."

Garry was the first of three show creators that I would work with who loved actors and went out of their way to protect us (Mitch Hurwitz of **Arrested Development** and Jill Soloway from **Transparent** are the other two). Our very first shot for **Larry Sanders** was a "walk and talk," which means all the actors walk together toward the camera as the cameraman, with the camera on his shoulder, walks backward. There was no cut, so everyone had to get all of the lines right. In that first scene, I believe it was Rip Torn, who had been cast as the show's producer, Artie; Jeremy Piven as the head writer Jerry;

Wallace Langham was another writer, named Phil; Linda Doucett as Hank's assistant Darlene; and me all walking this long corridor from the office all the way down to the bank of elevators.

My heart was absolutely pounding through my chest as we got ready to start.

And "Action!"

We all did our lines and made it to the elevator.

And "Cut!"

Garry turned and extended his arm to each of us one by one, openhanded, palm up, as if to say, **You okay? You okay? You okay? You okay? You okay?**

I thought, **O brave new world!**

I loved Hank. People called him a buffoon, and I never understood that. I thought he was very intelligent, and I protected him. And I'm sure he protected me.

Hank loved Larry, loved going to work. He owed Larry everything for rescuing him from a cruise ship and bringing him to this network show as an announcer. For Hank, it was nothing short of redemption. In the show, Hank protected Larry.

One of my favorite episodes of **The Larry Sanders Show** was one when Hank falls in love with Rabbi Marcy Klein (played by Amy Aquino), whom he meets after running into Marvin Hamlisch in front of his synagogue and Hamlisch invites Hank to services. Hank decides to give up "booze and cheap sex," and embrace his Jewish faith. Artie tells him to keep it to himself, but Hank insists on wearing the oversized white yarmulke Rabbi Klein gives him all the time, even on the air. In order to film the show-within-the show, the cameraman had to cut Hank off at the forehead. Then Hank gets his first piece of hate mail—the salutation was "Dear Jewhead." And that was the end of that. Hank immediately took the yarmulke off. He was so easily hurt, which I found very sweet about him. Hank had a big heart but he could also be petty and self-absorbed, which I also loved about him.

At one point during the first season, Garry and I had a huge falling-out over something really trivial. We both stayed up all night feeling terribly bad about it. But when we got to the set the next day, we had to film a scene in which our characters fight, so we both said, "Let's not make up until after the scene."

In truth, Garry "took me to school" about an

aspect of acting that was necessary for the show-within-the-show that was part of each episode—the **Tonight** show, if you will.

I rehearsed a lot. In those days, I was a little more control-freakish and less improvisational. So Garry took me aside and said, "Listen, this part you can't rehearse. This part you just have to let happen. Whatever you do is fine. Just let it hang. You don't have to deliver."

It doesn't have to be perfect. It was probably the best piece of advice I ever got: **Let it happen.**

So we didn't rehearse hard. We rehearsed loose—almost marking it, and waiting for it to happen spontaneously in front of the audience, on the night.

This proved to be game-changing in itself one day when we were in Larry's office rehearsing a pivotal scene in the sixth episode of the second season, called "The Hankerciser 200." One of the recurring issues with Hank from the very first episode was that he was always shilling for some product or another, and in this case the exercise machine that he endorsed was causing injuries. Hank had asked Larry's ex-wife to write an article about the product, but then, when things started to go wrong, he asked Larry to talk her out of it. Larry wouldn't do it. Instead he said to Hank, "What do you expect?"

Hank started to storm out, and the line was: "And

now I have to pay for the fact that you're back together with that bitch." But for some reason, I said "cunt" instead.

The room stopped.

It's still a word that throws you a little bit, but more so then, and yet, boom, Garry put it right in the script. I think I am the first person to say the c-word on television. But that was Garry. If something shook you, if it changed you, if it was real, he went for it. It never would have happened if Garry hadn't taught me "Let it happen."

He became one of my best teachers and mentors. He was the kindest of geniuses. I always thought comedy was sacred. It was not just about laughing and feeling better, it was about character and revealing—and I'd found someone who worked as though he believed that too.

We shot the talk-show-within-the-show once every month, shooting several episodes together. We would do a segment, I'd introduce Jim Carrey, walk offstage, put on another suit, walk back on, introduce Sting, do another episode, walk back off, change, do it again. We couldn't get a guest at the beginning, but once we got well known and the show started to have cachet, celebrities began to treat **The Larry Sanders Show** as if it were **The Tonight Show.**

It was during this part of the taping that Garry inadvertently taught me something even more precious about acting.

Like all "real" late-night hosts, Larry Sanders began each show-within-the-show with a mono-logue made up of jokes. Five minutes before taping, Garry, dressed in his suit, went backstage behind the set to review the cue cards that had the jokes on them for that episode. Adding to the verisimili-tude of the show, Garry even hired the actual Cue Card Guy from Johnny Carson's **The Tonight Show.**

The writers would gather alongside Garry as he looked at all the cards, which covered the entire wall. It became a sort of ritual. Everyone's face was mor-dant. There was no comedy in those faces as Garry pointed his index finger at the cards and said, "That one. That one. That one." He didn't laugh, nobody laughed. "That one. That one."

The first time I saw him do this, a light went off

in my head: **Well, there it is.** It was one of those moments where I thought, **I get it.** It wasn't about the jokes on the cards, it was about Garry. I was spellbound by whatever his process was. It was so in the moment, so spontaneous.

As a young actor, I would plan my performance in my office or in my room. I would get up the next day to shoot, and I would get in my car and will the world away. It was as if I had a body prophylactic on. I wanted nothing to affect me. I didn't want to talk to anybody. I didn't want anything. And when I got to whatever set I was working on, I presented this pristine, rehearsed, performed character. I didn't just learn my own lines, I learned everybody's lines. I showed up two and a half hours before curtain and ran through the entire play.

What Garry was doing was a revelation, just as it had been when I first saw him on **It's Garry Shandling's Show** years earlier. With Garry, you didn't hide; you brought the day—what was affecting you right then, right there—no hiding, you brought the "day." It was like the crossroads of jazz and existentialism, as composer Ben Sidran once said, by "being yourself in the moment" and "open to what comes next."

Every month when we taped the show-within-the-show, I'd ask someone on the crew to give me a heads-up when Garry was going to look at the cards. It changed my acting. My preparation changed. I still worked very hard, but it was different.

I learned so much so fast on that set. It was character, character, character. And it wasn't just Garry. There was the great Rip Torn, a walking acting lesson on my left, and Janeane Garofalo on my right, and Jeremy Piven straight ahead. It was an amazing time. For seven years, every time I walked on the set, I would always find this hilarious laughter going on.

It was the early days of HBO, and no one was making a great deal of money. Craft service, which was usually food for miles on a set, wasn't nearly so extravagant. One day there was nothing but coffee and Halls cough drops.

But somehow I knew this show was going to be a big hit. I just knew it would break the mold. And it did. It paved the way for shows like Larry David's **Curb Your Enthusiasm** and **The Office.** In fact, it wasn't just the faux documentary style of **The Office** that was a nod to Larry Sanders; Ricky Gervais has credited Hank Kingsley as a model for his character, David Brent.

And then it came to an end, as everything does. The two-part finale was designed to mimic Johnny Carson's famous farewell show. There was offstage backbiting about who would get to be the Bette Midler character (country star Clint Black, which caused a kerfuffle because a man shouldn't sing a love song to a man) and who would be the final guest—Jim Carrey was spectacular in his adulation on-camera and his loathing off-camera. Throughout the episode, Rip Torn's Artie is backstage losing the battle not to cry.

And just as Johnny did, the very last segment was Larry by himself sitting on a stool in front of the blue curtain, simply talking to the audience. Garry had asked me to sit in Hank's spot on the couch off-camera while he taped this last part. It was actually very moving and heartfelt, but Garry being Garry, he managed to get a sly joke in there. At the beginning of Larry's final speech, he looked back at me as he said, "You know, television is a risky business." Smiles, looks back at me. "You want to entertain. You want to try to do something new every night. You want to say something fresh. Nine times out of ten, you end up with **The Ropers.**" And then, after seven years of "No flipping" before a commercial break, he pronounced: "You can now flip."

The ending is famous, with Larry and Hank and

Artie first fighting, and then ending in a three-way embrace in the empty studio. But there was an alternate ending that I always loved. There was this idea that the final scene would show Larry doing something normal, outside the studio. So we filmed a scene with Larry and his girlfriend, played by Illeana Douglas, walking through a petting zoo. Larry sees a child eating something and says, "What's that?" And Illeana explains it's a hot dog. But the part I loved was when the camera pulls back to show Hank following at a distance, as though he simply couldn't bear to be separated from Larry. I know how he feels.

In my own career, there was before **The Larry Sanders Show,** and after **The Larry Sanders Show.** There would have been no **Arrested Development,** and there would have been no **Transparent.** Garry changed everything.


I had been writing this book for several months, recovering memories from childhood, my early acting days, my experiences on **Transparent** and **Arrested Development,** before I finally decided to focus on the influence that Garry Shandling had on me. There was no reason for saving him; my dragonfly mind, flitting from subject to subject, just hadn't landed on his lily pad yet. But on March 24, 2016, it did, and I sat down to write this chapter. About fifteen minutes after I closed my computer that day,

I received a call. During the hours that I had happily spent reliving and appreciating the seven years I spent under Garry's generous comedic light, he had experienced some kind of emergency that caused him to call 911. He was unconscious by the time an ambulance got to his home a few minutes later. I was still writing about him then.

Only a few weeks earlier, I had a wonderful thing happen when Garry and Judd Apatow came to the hotel where I was staying in L.A. The three of us had a great reunion, talking about the show and our memories of those days. After lunch, Judd took his leave and Garry and I walked to the Santa Monica green. We sat there, leaning on our elbows like the two old men in **I'm Not Rappaport,** and we talked for a couple of hours. We kept saying to each other, "It was special, wasn't it? It was a special time." Over and over we said it, variations on the theme of how special it was to us. Not that we were so special or that we were so good, but that those years on the set of **The Larry Sanders Show** were a very special time.

And then, a few hours after I had enjoyed the lovely memories of that special time, I was called on to make a public statement about his passing. What on earth could I say? There were no words to encompass what I had spent hours trying to encapsulate that same morning. Finally, I came up with something Twitter-friendly, as is the norm of the day. No thoughtful eulogies for our fallen heroes more than 140 characters (including spaces). So I said: "Garry was my dear friend and was and always will be my teacher. Garry redesigned the wheel of comedy and he was the kindest and funniest of Geniuses. I will miss him so much."

That doesn't begin to cover it. When I won a Golden Globe for my role as Maura in **Transparent** in 2015, Garry texted me and said, "I'm standing in my kitchen crying." Nobody was a bigger booster or more supportive than Garry. He changed my life.

Garry and I had another bond that we rarely talked about. We both had monstrous mothers, and we had both lost our brothers young. Garry was just ten years old when his older brother died of cystic fibrosis. His mother didn't even tell him; she said, "Your brother has gone to live with your grandmother."

In the nearly two decades after the end of **Larry Sanders,** people often asked, "What happened to Garry? How come he didn't do anything after that?" As though he had somehow failed. Garry did exactly what he wanted to do. He'd achieved something spectacular with **Larry Sanders;** he didn't need to do anything else. He had offers coming out his ears, including from me, and he turned them all down.

In fact, he was meticulous about the legacy of that show. He slaved over the DVD compilation, adding new material about how the show was put together, interviews with the cast, and even some of our audition tapes (including mine). He wasn't satisfied putting out a simple boxed set of all the episodes; he wanted the DVD set to be more than that. As one fan wrote of it, "This is totally different from anything I have seen."

In 2012, **Entertainment Weekly** brought the cast together for a twentieth-anniversary reunion shoot. Garry was two and a half hours late. When he arrived, he said, "Sorry, I just needed to find these props." He'd been searching for the Larry Sanders nameplate and coffee mug that had adorned his desk on the set during the show-within-the-show. He wanted to include them in the shoot. It was so Garry to care that much.

I took issue with the obituaries that said he left no survivors. Bullshit. He left thousands of survivors. He was his own man, but when another actor or comedian or musician came to him for advice or counsel or input on a script, he was there. So many writers have come up to me to say, "That was my favorite show. That was the show that made me want to write for television." A good number of writers have said, "The first script that I sent out to get a job was for **Larry Sanders**."

When I left that last lunch with Garry, I did something not unlike what I did on my way to my first audition for **The Larry Sanders Show**—I drove around. I drove and I drove, in circles, and all the while I was just thinking about our conversation and all the history and meaning it held. I don't know how long I'd been circling when I drove past Garry's car, and there was Garry, sitting in the driver's seat, not moving, not driving, just looking into the distance. I thought, **He feels it too. This conversation today was important. It changed him, too.**

I had no idea that would be the last time I would see him. I had no idea that the day I decided to write about my experience with Garry, what he did for me, for my acting, for the gift of Hank Kingsley, that it would be the same moment, or moments, that he left us. I believe that coincidences happen for a reason, and I think in Garry's passing through he may have taken a small detour by my house and whispered in my ear: **Let it happen.**

## 24

George Bluth, Sr. (file photo)

# Indictmer

## George and Oscar

I wasn't even supposed to be in the thing. I was originally what they call a day player on **Arrested Development,** who turned into a two-day player, then a three-day player, and then— voilà—into a regular recurring member of the cast.

I had known about the Bluths for some time. Mitch Hurwitz and I have been friends for years, and we hung out at the same Starbucks in Pacific Palisades (where coincidentally Maura Pfefferman would live some years later). The odd thing is, Mitch and I both had lovely homes where we had lovely, well-appointed, quiet offices, but somehow both he and I were drawn to the noisy confines of our local and hugely entitled coffee shop, he with his yellow legal pad and me with some script or other.

The first thing you notice about Mitch is that he has a big gorgeous face topped by a huge forehead. I quickly learned it has to be that big because he's so fucking bright. I honestly think he has two brains. And when Mitch has a "lock" on a project and is engaged, his eyes get wonderfully frenzied and he has this beatific, winning smile on his face. When Mitchie is writing, he beams with confidence and creativity, and just a little sweat on that big forehead.

Mitch and I worked on a show he created many years before called **Everything's Relative,** and Mitch wrote every episode himself. I played the dad character, and the magical Jill Clayburgh played my wife. It was a wonderful show coproduced by the mega-successful producing team of Paul Junger Witt and Tony Thomas, whose hits included the groundbreaking **Soap, Benson,** and **The Golden Girls.** I think everyone was a little surprised that, with all this firepower, the show lasted . . . wait for it . . . four episodes.

Mitch didn't hold it against me, and a couple of years later I got to do a big-screen romantic comedy with Jill, **Never Again,** so it was all good.

Anyway, one morning at our local Starbucks, Mitch told me about this family called the Bluths. I remember being secretly envious that I would not be a part of this glorious family, not only because he didn't offer it to me but also because I was under contract to CBS for a pilot that I had just shot, and I was waiting for it to be picked up or not. I was not excited about it; I believe I played a dentist, and dentists as a group are not intrinsically comic material. (Except for mine. Hi, Dr. Ford!)

**CUT TO:** In early 2003, I was getting off a plane in Los Angeles from Prague, where I had been shooting **Hellboy** with director Guillermo del Toro. They give you another phone when you're in Europe, so I hadn't used my normal phone while I was away. There was a slew of messages waiting for me, but one stood out: "Hi, it's Mitchie. Listen, pal, I'm wondering if you can come by. I'd love for you to do this thing for me."

He was about to shoot the pilot about the very Bluth family we had discussed months before, and he wanted me to play George Bluth Sr. The character was intended to be in the pilot only, so I'd only be needed for a couple of days. Obviously, I said yes.

There's a wonderful thing that happens when you know you're a day player. I think everyone should go to work every day thinking they're a day player. You

know that at the end of the day, you can go on to the
next job or you can go on safari. There's a certain
liberation to that. I was free as a bird. Also, the pilot
was written by Mitch, and George Sr. was arguably
one of the funniest characters ever dreamed up.

My very first scene was George Sr.'s retirement
party on the boat. The first thing I had to do was
welcome everybody and announce George's successor as CEO of the Bluth Company. I was wearing
sunglasses and a Stetson, and Jason Bateman was
standing right in front of me. There was a band,
and the drummer kept drumming when the director yelled, "Action!" He wouldn't stop, so I yelled,
"Hey, hey, fuckhead!" (This was not part of the
scene, in case you're looking for it on Netflix.) I
looked over at Jason's face. He was beaming.

That day, I met all the actors who played the
Bluth children: Jason, Tony Hale, Portia de Rossi,
and Will Arnett, and the son-in-law played by David
Cross. Will is one of the funniest and most droll
human beings ever created. Portia was extremely

nice, and she was very touchy-feely with me, and I thought, **Oh my gosh. She's coming on to me**.

(I'll pause while you laugh.)

Men are idiots. They are a lower species. I thought she was all over me. I have never admitted this before now, not even to Portia. Hi, Portia! (Hi, Ellen!)

Here's the really embarrassing part. This wasn't the first time this happened to me. Back in the mid-'80s, I did an episode of **The Twilight Zone** with Helen Mirren, one of our greatest actresses and one of our greatest human beings. In one scene, we were to kiss. When the director yelled, "Action!" we kissed. And oh, what a kiss. It was very passionate. "Cut!" I walked over to my chair in a state. **This is horrible. What are we going to say to Taylor Hackford? Helen is obviously in love with me. This is going to be so difficult. What am I going to do?** It made no impression on me that Helen was sitting next to me as we were waiting to resume shooting and didn't speak to me. Thirty minutes— not one word. When we set up the next shot—and "Action!"—she kissed me again. **Do we talk to somebody?**

Finally it hit me. **Oh my God, she's acting.**

Again, lower species. Hi, Helen.

Anyway, back on the boat, I remember looking out and seeing David Cross as Lindsay's husband, Tobias, wearing one of her frilly blouses for his pirate costume on a neighboring boat filled with gay men staging a protest about gay marriage at sea. It was so out of left field, I thought, **Whatever this is, I need to be a part of it**.

I went over to David Nevins—who is now the head of Showtime but he was with Ron Howard's production company, Imagine Entertainment, then—and told him how much I loved the show. I got a sense that there was some murmuring backstage about my continuing in my role, but I was still waiting to hear about the non-hilarious-dentist show.

In the meantime, I returned to Prague to shoot the rest of **Hellboy.**

Late one night in my hotel room, my cell phone rang. It was my agent, Leslie Siebert at Gersh, calling to tell me two things:

"Your series did not get picked up."

"Yes!" I shouted.

"**Arrested** wants you."

"Yes!" I shouted even louder.

"How many do you want to do?"

"How many are they doing?"

"Thirteen."

"I want to do thirteen!" I may have screamed.

So we made a deal. (I found out later that an executive at Fox said, "This moves forward with Jeffrey and David Cross," who had also been hired just for the pilot.) My first year on that show consisted of driving over to the Fox movie studios, taking off my street clothes, putting on an orange jumpsuit, and filming. During the second episode, I was doing a prison scene in my jumpsuit and I'd added a black do-rag. "I love it here!" I said, shaking hands with a prisoner passing by. I looked over at Jason. Jason is like my son. I love Jason. **I think there's something up with Jason.** We were doing the scene, and I couldn't shake it: he was staring at my forehead during the entire scene. **He has some sort of affliction.** With every take, he did the same thing. **What is going on?**

He later confessed to me that it was the only way he could stop himself from laughing at George Sr.'s antics. We were bonded for life.

It was such a funny, edgy show. Just as Garry Shandling had given the audience credit, so too did Mitch. **Arrested** wasn't just funny, it was smart. When David's character was a Blue Man, he walked through the house in one scene, and then in a later scene you'd see a little smudge of blue on the wall where he'd been earlier. It was the kind of touch that made people hit Rewind.

And George Sr.? Well, they just don't come more Darwinian. He would do anything—anything—to survive, even making himself look like Saddam Hussein and burying himself in the ground. I remember people on the film crew stifling their laughter as they lowered me into the ground and poured dirt over me, and I was giggling beneath the sand. I mean, who gets a job like this? Who gets to play catch with his son (Will) in a prison yard, both of us dressed in orange jumpsuits? Who gets to burn himself on a cornballer while doing a commercial? Or do a "chicken dance" joined by the whole family to humiliate his son? Or dress up as a Blue Man like his son-in-law to escape detection? (I was picking blue things from mysterious places in my body for weeks after shooting that scene.)

And who gets to do work like this twice in a lifetime? First **The Larry Sanders Show,** then **Arrested Development**? Just one of those would have been, as my grandpa would have said, **dayenu.**

**Arrested** turned into an embarrassment of riches when Oscar Bluth was born. Now I had two characters on the show. And Oscar was a testament to the creative genius of Mitch and the writing staff.

When we did flashback scenes to George's hirsute younger days, I had to wear a wig. The makeup department had bought a cheap Darnell wig for me that a balding homeless person would have thrown away, so I insisted on a better one. They had a good one woven especially for the show. Here's the thing with wigs, in case you've never had one: they don't cut them. So the new wig went down to my shoulders. The makeup trailer was right next to the writers' building, so when I tried it on, I stepped outside the trailer and looked up to the fourth floor balcony where Mitch was looking down at me. We asked him what length he wanted to cut it.

"Hold on a second," he said, and called the writers out. There must have been fifteen of them all looking down at me.

As Mitch turned to go back to his office, he yelled down, "Don't cut it," and that was when George's brother, Oscar Bluth, was born. George didn't have a twin brother until that moment. That was the kind of electric spontaneity that show had, where the script could change on a dime. It was very freeing.

That's not to say that the writing was easy. Every

once in a while I'd wander over from the sound-stage to the writers' building to chat with Mitch or just grab a cup of coffee. I once saw Mitch and Jim Vallely, a dear friend of mine and a trusted compatriot of Mitch's, in Mitch's office where they were "breaking" a story. Mitch was lying on the couch, his right arm behind his head. Jim was standing over him with pencil and paper. Their discussion was very quiet and intense, and I realized that what seemed to flow so effortlessly from them was actually like a birth. There was enormous concentration in what they were doing. It was a total revelation to me.

Often people asked me, "You just made that up on the fly, right?" It was actually a very tightly scripted show, with little ad-libbing. The only time I remember doing it, in fact, was on that first day of shooting, before I knew I'd be a member of the cast. Mitch had this idea that I should get on the phone with my secretary as the SEC Boats approach to arrest George Sr. The call wasn't in the script, so I just said to dead air, "Burn it, save it, burn it, save it. Why are **you** crying?" As a result of that call, the character of George Sr.'s secretary, Kitty Sanchez (played by Judy Greer), was born.

With great wisdom comes great silliness, and Mitch wasn't afraid to be completely silly. The character Bob Loblaw? **Bob Blah blah?** Give me a break, that's genius.

The one thing that was challenging for the cast was the timing of the script delivery each week. This was back in the days when scripts would be delivered to actors' houses, cars leaving various production offices to drive all over Hollywood in the middle of the night so that the script would be in your mailbox or by your door when you woke up. Normally, you'd have a script at least a day or two before filming, maybe even a week. Mitch was writing right up to the last minute, so we usually didn't get the scripts until the morning of shooting, which meant you prayed your scene wasn't first up that day so you had a few hours to learn your lines. For some reason, I think it was Portia who usually led off. My Portia.

It was searingly intense making a show like this. The creation of something so wonderfully funny is very serious work, and we all took it very seriously. If you didn't, woe unto you.

One week, my regular makeup person was out, and I had a substitute. After each shot, the makeup people would come over and touch you up. When the sub came over to me after the first "Cut," she made that sad trombone sound **wah-wah-wah.** (Think Rachel Dratch's Debbie Downer character on **SNL.**)

"What are you doing?"

"Oh, you know, that's the end of the scene," she said.

"You can never make that sound to me again," I said. "Ever."

"What's the big deal?"

"This is hard," I said.

We did another scene—"Cut!"—she came over to pat me down. **"Wah-wah-wah."**

Clearly, not a lot of support here.

"Why? Why are you doing this?"

Another scene, another scene, she kept doing it.

"You have to go," I finally said. I couldn't have someone who didn't get it.

Silly is not for the timid. Think: Steve Allen, David Letterman, Mel Brooks, Gene Wilder, Gilda Radner, Richard Pryor, Ernie Kovacs, John Belushi, Tina Fey, Amy Poehler, Amy Schumer—and you get where I'm going. Silly is an exalted line that goes all the way back to Aristophanes, and it's to be respected and it needs support. As Grandpa would say, "It's not for **pishers.**"

The show was so strong, such a trailblazer, but the audience numbers didn't reflect how popular the show really was, so we went the way of all television shows and were canceled after three seasons.

Until we came back for Season Four—**years** later. Thanks to the genius of Mitch Hurwitz, I may well be playing George and Oscar Bluth until I'm dead. Or maybe after. Well, certainly after. I mean, streaming is eternal, right?

## 25

This is me.

# Waiting for Maura

People say to me, "You must be having the best time of your life." And I say, "Yes." What I don't say is it can also be very hard because I get into a bit of a state when I play Maura. It would be wrong to say "nervous," because I'm not scared, or not "performer scared." The word that comes to mind is "cranky." It's bad mood–adjacent, just a bit north of "grumpy." And it's because I am obsessed with doing Maura right.

It's like having a rope around your neck. When I'm away from the set, the rope is very loose, but I know the rope is there. If I have a 10:00 a.m. call, the rope begins tightening at 7:00 a.m. when I wake up. It's tighter by 8:00 a.m. when I have yogurt; 8:30, granola, tighter. By the time my assistant, Van Barnes, picks me and the vultures up for the ride to the set, I can't talk. Van thinks I'm just being actory and preparing, but I'm actually just asking myself, **Can I pull this off again?** Every day I drive past the Paramount gates, I get in that mood. I get uncomfortable. And it's the ideal mindset, because that discomfort is exactly how Maura feels every day. This is the most successful I've ever been, and it's the most antsy I've ever been. At the same time, I love playing Maura from "Action" to "Cut."

It began on a Thursday in July 2013. I flew to L.A. to appear on an interview show called **The Talk.** In the car from LAX to the Fairmont Hotel, where I always stay when I'm in town, I opened an e-mail from my agent, Leslie Siebert. She'd attached a script for the pilot of a new series written by Jill Soloway. "Look at Mort/Maura," she said. "This is a game changer." The last time she said that was when she told me I had been cast in **The Larry Sanders**

**Show.** Another game changer? Mort/Maura—what the . . . ?

I believe it was on page eight—a scene about eating barbecue—as my car was passing Whole Foods on Lincoln Boulevard, that I said to myself, "Oh my God." Game changer? I had never read anything like this before—a family whose patriarch comes out as a woman? The Pfeffermans are West Coast Jews who put the **d** back in dysfunctional. You could describe the Tambors of Westlake the same way.

I called Leslie as soon as I got to my room. "I'm in. Tell them I'm in."

"Well, you have to meet Jill Soloway."

"Fine, whatever, I'm in."

The next day I did my segment on **The Talk,** a CBS show filmed in the Valley. I arranged to meet Jill right after that at a Le Pain Quotidien right around the corner from **The Talk** on Ventura Boulevard. I walked in and Jill met me at a table and told me to wait just a bit as she finished up with a reporter who was interviewing her for **Afternoon Delight,** for which she had won the directing prize at the Sundance Film Festival. While she was telling me this, the first thing that hit me over the head was Jill's eyes. There is such a presence, and they shine and go deep. There is just no doubt that she sees, that she is a seer.

When she was done, she came over to my table and sat down to talk. She showed me pictures of her parent, Carrie, who had recently come out as trans and was the inspiration for the show.

This is how the conversation went:

Jill said a sentence, and I said, "I'm in."

Jill said another sentence, and I said, "I'm in."

Jill said another sentence, and I said, "I'm in."

I all but threw myself at her, because this script of hers had struck me in much the way I'd been struck by **The Larry Sanders Show** and **Arrested Development.** In all three, there were risk and great characters and great writing. All three also shared a nontraditional platform: **Larry Sanders** was one of the first original shows on HBO, **Arrested** was one of the first original shows on Fox, and now **Transparent** was going to be a streaming show on Amazon—it's television that isn't even on television.

But this show had so much more, because Mort Pfefferman becomes one of the most fantastic people I have ever encountered—Maura Pfefferman.

"I'm in."

I put my hand up to high-five her, and she put up hers but stopped. "Not quite yet," she said. "Give me a little time." Was there another actor in line ahead of me? I had no idea. I still have no idea. And no, never tell me, ever.

I went back to my room at the hotel and watched a copy of **Afternoon Delight** that Jill had sent me. I loved it. I could see that Jill never rushed a moment; she let a moment play all its truth. Her director of photography was the brilliant Jim Frohna, and she was bringing him on board for **Transparent.** I loved the film's star, the great Kathryn Hahn, who plays Rabbi Raquel in **Transparent.**

I called Jill (in the same way I called Garry Shandling years earlier) and left a message telling her how floored I was and "I'm in." We swapped a few e-mails. Days passed.

Finally, my agent called. **Yes!** "Jill wants you for **Transparent.**" YES!

And here was a bonus: among my amazing co-stars was my friend from the Milwaukee Rep more than forty years before, Judith Light.

I flew out to L.A. two weeks before we were to begin shooting the pilot. Kasia and the kids stayed in New York.

Our first table read was on the Paramount Studios lot. There were no nameplates, no scripts premarked in yellow, but there was this: Jill Soloway seated at the head of the table. "I want to make the world safe for my parent." With that mission statement, the actors began—as Neil Young would sing it—and that baby lifted right off the ground. It sailed and soared, and it ended with a trio of three actresses accompanied by a lone guitar singing "Operator" by Jim Croce: "Operator, well could you help me place this call?"

As the music came to an end, there wasn't a dry eye in the house. There was silence, and then the room burst into applause that lasted forever. I was sitting next to Judith, and we looked at each other. We had just witnessed the best table read of our careers.

But there were a lot of days I spent alone— not lonely, but alone. I had rented a bungalow in Pacific Palisades. It was very small, with just the fundamentals—sofa, table, chairs, all covered with the first drafts of Season One. I was paralyzed in the face of the daunting task and season ahead of me. There were friends in the Palisades—I used to live there back in the day—but I couldn't pick up the phone. It was just me, the bungalow, and all the scripts from Season One of **Transparent.**

One night my friends Jay and Julia Phelan invited me to dinner at a local restaurant, but during the meal I realized I couldn't understand what they were talking about and I was unable to talk. I saw them stealing looks at each other. That was my last night in public till filming. I hadn't found Maura, nor did I have the technique of playing Maura or really know what I was doing. I took me and my paralysis back to our bungalow.

I met with Jenny Boylan, Zackary Drucker, and Rhys Ernst, my trans teachers. How do I, Jeffrey Tambor, how do I do this? This is not putting on clothes, or getting a mani-pedi. This is a transition to another life. How do you do it right?

All of this Sturm und Drang, the shaky hands, became a godsend, an unintentional way to Maura. She too is alone—not lonely, but alone—she too has shaky hands. She too doesn't know how to do Maura; she just has to. She has no choice.

I remember dropping my kids off at a French summer camp in Montreal, and as I was leaving I turned and saw Gabriel sitting by himself eating his awful dinner, and the table came up to his nose. We got in the car, and Kasia drove while I blubbered. The reason I was blubbering is, I am that kid. And that's the universality of Maura. There's alone and there's **alone.**

Then Jill arranged a field trip for a few of us to a bar in the Valley called the Oxwood. It would be Maura's debut. Jill, Jim Frohna, Rhys Ernst, and Zackary Drucker came to my room—609, Fairmont Hotel, Santa Monica, to be forever called the Maura Suite (I stay there still)—and we talked a long time. They helped make me up and dress as Maura. I remember her coming to life in the mirror and meeting my new friend for the first time. She

looked nice, friendly, rather pretty, and a bit shy—
she kept averting her glance.

I walked unsteadily through the hotel lobby to
the car. I thought, **Don't ever forget this feeling
because this is every day of Maura's life.** My new
friend and I were "stepping out."

When I got out of the car in front of the bar, the
valet said, "Do you know who's here tonight? Judith
Light!"

I walked in and Maura was welcomed by everyone there. It wasn't about Jeffrey, it was about her.
The staff knew what we were doing, and they were
incredibly supportive. We all danced that night—
Jill, Judith, Rhys, Zackary, Jim, and Maura.

When I needed to use the bathroom, Judith said,
"Where are you going to go?"

"I'm going to the ladies' room."

"Do you want me to come with you?" she asked
and started to follow.

"No, I'm going to go on my own."

I took Maura on another field trip, to Gelson's Market, because I thought that's where she would do her grocery shopping. I stood in the middle of an aisle thinking, **What would Maura eat?** Another shopper looked at me and smirked. It was one of the meanest smirks I've ever seen. **Oh my God.** I had been clocked. **So that's what** that **feels like. Don't forget this feeling.**

Zackary and I got a couple of salads to eat in the seating area outside the store. There were no free tables, so Zackary pointed toward one where a man was seated talking on his cell phone.

"No," I said.

"Go," Zackary said.

We sat down and the man kept talking, glancing up at us every once in a while. He finished his call and stood up. "Have a good day, ladies," he said and walked away.

Zackary beamed and immediately high-fived me as I spiritually flew around the world.

I was throw-up nervous before my first scene on the first day of shooting, but it turned out to be a love fest. I will forever remember sitting around the round dinner table with the actors who play the Pfefferman children: Gaby Hoffmann, Amy Landecker, and Jay Duplass, all of our faces smeared with barbecue sauce, and just offscreen are Jill Soloway and Jim Frohna behind the camera. Everywhere I looked—there was genius holding down the fort. **Whatever this is, this is home base.**

In that first scene, I was playing Mort, and Mort is about to tell his children his secret. I put my head down and said this line that I adore, "I love you guys love you guys love you guys." I barely whispered it, and when I looked up, I saw this powerful table—Amy to my left, Gaby to my right, and Jay opposite. It was in that moment that I said to myself, **This thing is going to go.**

The pilot was done, and I returned to my life in New York to wait. When we got picked up for ten episodes and I returned to L.A. to shoot the season, I had to confront something: I had to build and embody Maura, a transgender character. I am a cisgender male. I was seventy years old. I'd never played a trans character. I thought I knew a lot about the trans community, but I knew nothing. I was certain that there would come a day when there would be a tapping on my dressing room door and someone saying, "I'm sorry, we made a terrible mistake. We're going another way."

Shortly before the first season aired, Jill screened the first couple of episodes at the Directors Guild of America. I sat behind a trans woman who was flipping through her program rapidly and dismissively and saying, "Oh! Oh!" When the lights came down and the show started, she didn't watch. She put her head down. Growing up in that house where the corridors were filled with danger, I got good at sensing when something was amiss. The whole energy field around this woman was not good. I remember elbowing my assistant Van Barnes and nodding toward the row in front of us. "Something bad this way comes."

When the lights came up after the screening, Jill and I and the rest of the cast took the stage for a panel discussion and Q&A with the audience. After some very nice questions and answers, the "Oh! Oh!" woman stood up and—**Here it comes.** And indeed it came. Eileen and Barney grabbed the microphone. "This is like watching blackface. What is he doing in this role? A transgender actress should be playing Maura."

Jill and Zackary handled the situation artfully, but I went into a fugue state all the way back to Daly City, California. **Shtick drek. Shhhhh . . . shhhhh. Keep your nose clean, Beppy. Don't make waves . . . shhhhhh.**

When we left the stage, people were saying words of congratulation to me but I couldn't hear, I could just see mouths moving. My friend Peter Binazeski, who is the head of publicity for Amazon, had to put me in my car. I recovered by Season Three, but I feel that **tap tap tap** every day when we're shooting, still.

**Do this right. Do this right. Do this right.**

Much of the show, and of my effort to embody Maura, is figuring out where she belongs. Once she comes out as a woman, she can't go back. She can only go forward; but what does forward look like? Is it femme? Is it Mother Earth? Is it maidenly? Is it sexy? Is she going to take hormones? How does she talk? How do you wear lipstick? How do you walk in heels? What does she look like? Who are her friends? Will she be loved? Will she be able to love?

This show is a revelation not just in what it addresses but in the alchemy Jill Soloway brings to it. Jill has the lightest and yet deepest touch of any director I have worked with. She is actor-centric and understands what an actor does and what an actor has to do to get to the truth of a scene. Under her baton exists the safest, most innovative set I have ever been on. There are no mistakes, there's just another take, a different take.

One morning, Gaby Hoffmann and I got to the set early to do a scene together. When we arrived, there was Jill, all scrunched up in her parka (sound-stages can get very cold), with her eyes closed, thinking. I could tell she had gotten to the set earlier than all of us and had been there for a while, imagining the scene to come. She wasn't blocking it or story-boarding it, she was simply imagining it.

She runs an intuitive set where things can change on a dime. In Season One, on what happened to be my seventieth birthday, we were doing a Shabbos candle-lighting scene that is interrupted by Sarah's husband (played by the wonderful Rob Huebel), who is furious that she is in a lesbian relationship with another woman, and Maura lets him have it. It was going very well, and then Jill came on the set and whispered in my ear a complete reversal of what we were doing. She prompted me to have not a masculine reaction, as I was naturally inclined to, but a woman's reaction—gentler, inclusive, more befitting Maura than Jeffrey. And yet she didn't tell me what to do, there was no "direction" in the conventional sense. She was adding ingredients and taking away others, in the process changing Maura's mind. At the end of the next take, Jill didn't yell, "Cut!" She simply walked up to me and kissed me on the cheek. Then she led me down the corridors of the Pfefferman house set, turn left here, right there, until we reached the final door. Through it, in the vast arena of the soundstage, was a huge birthday cake, every member of the production team, and Carrie, Jill's real-life Moppa, ready to sing "Happy Birthday."

Another day, another scene, another Jewish ritual, this time Yom Kippur, and again all the Pfeffermans are seated around the huge table. It is revealed that Shelly had had a miscarriage years ago. Once again, it was going very well, and then, **walk walk walk,** here comes our Jill, who whispers something very quickly, not even fifteen seconds, into the ear of Judith Light, or as I like to call her, "Killer" (because she murders a scene). On the next take, there came from Judith such a mournful keening it could only have sprung from the underworld. Whatever Jill whispered to her elicited this performance.

Jill isn't only about her direction; she encourages us to be in the moment on the set. In the first episode of Season Two, Maura's older daughter, Sarah, is marrying Tammy. The entire family, all dressed in white, gathers for a wedding photograph. Maura asks the photographer, "Do you want my head up or head down?" And the photographer says, "I think chin up for you, sir." It was a mistake, but with the freedom we're given by Jill, I went with it. I said to Judith/Shelly, "Did he just call me 'sir'?"

"Yes."

"We're done. We're done." And Shelly and Maura walk off. It was entirely unintended, but it was a spectacular way to open the episode. Amazon used it in the publicity for the season, all because Jill fearlessly didn't yell "Cut!" In fact, I distinctly remember the sound of Jill's laugh from all the way over in the video village where she was watching the action on screen. It was Jack Cook all over again.

By the third season, Maura had infiltrated my life. Sometimes when I'm talking, I hear her. Even in my daily word choice. I wear Maura's ring on my pinky even when I'm not working on the show. And I do use the ladies' room probably more often than I should. I am known for walking into women's bathrooms in airports all over the country until someone says, "Excuse me, sir?" That difference no longer exists to me. There was one episode that season when I had to play young Mort, and I had no idea how to do it. I felt false and actory, because this wasn't who this character was anymore.

One day, my daughter Evie said, "Dad, I want to go to the set."

Kasia and I looked at each other.

"Uh . . . er . . . see, um, Daddy's playing a . . ."

She got right to it. She was nine years old. "Daddy, I understand. I know that the character is more comfortable as a woman." Out of the mouths of babes.

I took her to the set. She sat next to me and watched as Daddy put his makeup on and was transformed into Maura. And then my daughter and I had a mani-pedi together.

On the morning of the first day of shooting Season Three, Jill got up on a box and gathered the entire cast and crew together to address us. People streamed out of offices to gather on the stage. When Jill was done, I said a few words. Then, one by one, other people got up on the box and said something. It was profound, the inclusivity of this group. Someone said, "We should do this every morning." And so we did. The beginning of each day began with a chorus of people yelling, "Box!"

The day Prince died, DJ, one of our camera operators, talked about how important Prince had been to him. Everyone on that set was affected, across generations, from me down to the **pishers.** Then Jill said, "Can someone in Sound put on some Prince?" The music came on and everyone started dancing. I said to a PA, "Mark this moment, because you will never see this again." You will never see this on any set where fear reigns, where there's not enough time, there's not enough money, there's no sense of play, where everyone is worried about being canceled and billing and the size of their dressing room. On this set Jill has, everyone is wearing a red bowtie.

The final episode of Season Three (spoiler alert) takes place on a cruise ship. There's not enough Xanax or Ambien to persuade me to take a cruise. I was certain I would die on this cruise. I mean, I did **The Love Boat.** Why would I ever get back on a cruise ship?

I fucking loved it. I had my own little cabin and my own butler. The one concession we had to make shooting on the boat was that we had to dress and do makeup in our cabins. My butler was from the Philippines, so he had zero idea of who I was. What he did know was that sometimes when he brought the breakfast rolls, Mr. Tambor would be in full Maura costume and wig. One time he walked in when my assistant Van was on her knees painting my toenails.

Anyway, the cruise ship was perfect for me. My whole life, I've loved two things. I love to be by myself, but know that people are nearby. The ship outside the door of my little private cabin was filled with thousands of people. I would leave my cabin and take the elevator to the deck where we were filming. Some days on that elevator, I was dressed as a man. Others, as a woman. The looks on the passengers' faces when I was in full Maura were amazing. Van and I laughed very hard after some of those elevator rides.

The other thing I love is knowing that food is there. I don't want to eat the food because I have a fear of gaining weight ("Look how you look"), but I need to know it's there. On the ship, there was food everywhere. It's in your shoes. They put it in your toothpaste. You walk out of your cabin and there's food. My butler brought me sandwiches every day. I never ate them, but I was so happy the sandwiches were there. Then you go down to the dining hall and there are choices as far as the eye can see. I would walk around the room to the Asian station to watch them cook pot stickers, to the German station for the sausages, then to the BBQ and the pizza. I didn't eat any of it, but I felt joy because I love the kitchen. The kitchen makes me think of my grandma, and I associate it with creativity. For me, cooking is like acting, putting together ingredients until they become art. I'm addicted to **The Great British Bake Off;** I could watch it on a loop. Hi, Mary Berry! Bye, Mary Berry!

My crowning achievement during that week at sea was getting my photograph taken with the captain of the ship while wearing a captain's hat. In a nutshell, forty years of my career bracketed by cruise ships, from fourth billing after Sylvia the Seal on **The Love Boat** to **Transparent.** From shame to fame.

Judith Light asked me during a panel we did together at the Paley Center in New York, "What has changed for you since **Transparent**?"

"Aside from my tendency to use the ladies', I find myself getting cranky easily. It's like when you have a tag on your neck that scratches you."

"You mean like old people get?"

"Not a skin tag! A tag on your shirt!"

One day when we were filming, I was sitting in a stall in the women's room right off stage 15 at Paramount. I'd already peed, so I was just sitting there collecting my thoughts when two women from production came in. "It's going very well," I heard one of them say. "I'm glad he's in a good mood today."

I waited for a beat, and then: "I'm in here."

They hightailed it out of there. I probably should have kept my mouth shut. I guess I wanted to acknowledge that I knew that they knew that Maura could make me cranky.

See, here's the thing about acting. When a dog dies in most people's lives, you're sad. When you're an actor and the dog dies, you're sad and your acting gets better. In my case, my friend Garry died while we were filming the third season, and that passing knocked down any emotional barriers I had. It gave me more access.

And following Garry's orders, I "let it happen."

As I said to the crew during that lovely seventieth birthday party, this is what I always thought acting was supposed to feel like. All I ever wanted to do was this.

People like to use words like **authentic.** It's all around social media, posted on Facebook, tweeted around the word at Mach speed. But for the character of Maura, those words are her daily life. She has lived a lie for seventy years, **not** authentic, and alone and full of shame. That lie has made her see the world very clearly; she knows friend or foe immediately. Even after she comes out and begins to live her "true self," she struggles to find her place in the world.

But here's the deal—another "lie," if you will: at

the end of the day, I take my wardrobe off, hang it up, take off the makeup and nail polish (most days I leave it on), and put on my cisgender costume and head home to resume that life. I am an actor—I have been an actor for fifty years—and I have been trying to play Maura for only three seasons now. We have just been renewed for a fourth season as I am writing this book. Hi, Amazon! Hi, Jeff Bezos! Hi, Roy Price! Hi, Joe Lewis!

That said, I don't pretend to know the real-life transgender experience. As I said at the 2016 Emmys ceremony, I hope I am the last cisgender male to play a trans role. There is a wonderful pool of trans acting talent, and their journey needs to be acknowledged and honored. Roles need to be created and auditions need to be had.

Back in 1966, when I taught my first beginners' acting workshop at Wayne State as part of my scholarship to the graduate program, I had no idea what I was doing so I made up the class on the fly. The administration had given me a book from which to teach, but there is no book on acting. Mr. Mackley and Jack Cook didn't use a book. I flipped through the chapters and came to a section on comedy—seriously? There was a paragraph that outlined the sound of an audience's laughter from the beginning of an actor's line to the end of the laugh. There was a point on the curve where the performer was supposed to come "in." I took the book off the syllabus, which caused if not a furor in the department, certainly a "furette" and an academic "harrumph," and earned me a great deal of static from the bookstore. Already I was an outlier.

On the first day of this first acting class, my friend Dave Regal sat in the back row of the Studio Theater and smiled as he watched me twisting in the wind. Hi, Dave! The first thing I did was have the students lie on the ground. I have no idea why I did this; probably to give me time to think of something. I moved among the bodies on the floor and talked to them about following impulses and how important intuition is to being an actor. I talked about the danger of squelching impulses and trying to please people. Meanwhile, there was no book and a teacher new to Detroit was quite literally making the class up on the fly.

The world was in turmoil at the time. People were in the streets protesting the Vietnam War. I was out there too, on Woodward Avenue. The distrust of the government and a sense of fear were palpable in the air. You could see it in the faces on campus. I could feel it in this workshop. I was trying inexpertly to say to my students that here, in this room, they were safe. I promised them all passing grades and respect. (Indeed, I gave A's to everyone who even walked through the door.)

I looked down at a young woman, Dede Cavanaugh, and she was weeping. I wasn't at all sure of what I was saying, but her tears were the first sign that whatever the fuck I was talking about was somewhere near a truth. My friend Dave in the back had lost the smirk; he was sitting up and waiting to see what I was going to say or do next. As was I.

One by one, the students walked up on the stage and started talking to me. I had told them to bring a poem or something to read or a piece of art to show. When they were in "performance," I would interrupt and ask questions. **Where were you born? What's your home life like? What are your parents like?** When they resumed the performance, it would ineffably change into something very specific and human. I was getting them off "performance" and getting them onto the source—themselves. That made them "real." I have used this opening technique for fifty years, both with **pishers** and the veterans with multi-paged résumés.

**CUT TO:** The LGBT Center in Los Angeles, spring 2016. Some of the cast and crew of **Transparent** were invited to talk to people in the trans community and sign up people to work as background artists for the third season we were about to shoot. It was late afternoon, and I was seated at the **Transparent** table, shaking hands, taking pictures. In that afternoon, my Maura education was rebooted. This wasn't soundstage 21 at Paramount, this was a real center with real people from this community, trans men and women in every size and shape and stage of transition.

I kept waiting to be called out for my performance, as I had been at the DGA screening, for my entitled cisgender actor status, but I was welcomed and embraced. It really was a community—a revelation to me—and I wanted in. Just like I said to Jill, "I'm in."

Zackary Drucker, who is **my** teacher, and I arranged to do an acting workshop at the Center while I was in Los Angeles shooting Season Three. Before the first session, I told the class to bring in a personal monologue—the same assignment I have been giving my acting students for years.

I've noticed something that happens to me when I teach. My life gets better. I get better. Not my acting per se, but my life. It's what Milton and other teachers had said to me: when you teach, you're basically talking to yourself.

But I've also noticed that I always become angry—no, furious—on the drive to class. I think it has something to do with how much opposition there is in learning. The more years I teach, the more I can feel the opposition, and the more I fume in my car on the way.

When I enter the theater, and especially when I am in a critique with students, I can sense how many people there are in the space. It can get crowded; there are whole families surrounding each student—invisible fathers, mothers, aunts, uncles, lovers—and they are there because they've been unconsciously invited by the student.

My first Saturday at the LGBT Center was a miracle. As I walked in, I could feel it immediately, an urgent sense of need, more than I have ever felt anytime anywhere in all my years of teaching. And no opposition. Most of the students I taught wanted to get a pilot for a TV show. I once told an actor that I'd rather he become a pilot than get a pilot. (He actually became a pilot. Hi, Travis!) But in that small dark theater at the Center, the students were there to claim their right to be artists.

To be an actor, I believe, you have to be personal and you must act as if your life depends on it. These students were there because their lives depended on it. And let me repeat: There was no opposition. They were unattended by naysayers and family members. They had been "alone" for some time now. They weren't hoping to get a pilot, they **were** the pilots, and they were flying solo on this journey.

One by one, each student got up onstage and told their story.

For those hours in that room, I got to know who they were, and got to know who I was. That's the tightrope and the baton you hold to steady yourself, what I'd been training for my whole life. Acting and comedy are about saving lives. My dad used to say, "Be useful." This was useful.

When I teach—and it's an old, old habit—I keep all the lights on in the theater. I want to make sure we all understand we are in a classroom and we are working. There is no verisimilitude of "reality"; this is really happening. I like to sit somewhere on the side between performer and audience so I can keep an eye on both, because performance happens onstage, but the story takes place, finally, in the theater.

During the trans talent workshop, I could see Zackary on the left side of the theater smiling and giving me overt nods as the class and I were moving forward, and on the right side was Ali Liebegott—writer, actor, standup comic, and producer of **Transparent**—nodding along as if at prayer.

At the end of the first session at 4:00 p.m., I backed out of the LGBT Center parking lot, drove around the block, and stopped my car on the side of the street. I just stared ahead, just as I had after my final lunch with Garry. It was all in that room—all sorts of thoughts and images going off in my head: purpose—art—sealed orders—bowties—**This, This—Yes, Yes, Please**—all swirling around. I sat there for what seemed forever.

There was this one image I couldn't square with. She sat in the back that first day. She was very young-looking, probably in her twenties, and wearing a black shirt, jean jacket, and pants. Every time I looked her way, she would look away. I'm pretty good at reading people, and I couldn't read her.

At the next class I asked her to take the stage. When she got up to do her monologue, she talked about living at home with her father. She said that to get to this class, she left the house without telling her father where she was going. She changed her clothes and put on her wig in the car.

And there it was. My mind snapped into gear and changed course. I finally got it in corporeal form: this was, and is, the movement, standing in front of me. During the course of our workshop, she came out to her dad. She changed me.

The last monologue of the final class, a woman took the stage. She was in her sixties, very well dressed and coifed. She was the CEO of a company, and she drove two hours to get to the class. She was articulate, very smart, and had obviously been through a lot and emerged brilliantly as this woman speaking in front of us, leading us gently by the hand through her world as a trans woman in business. As she talked, I thought, **That's me.** That's what I'm trying to create in **Transparent.** That's Carrie, Jill's real-life Moppa. She could have been Maura.

I was teaching her, but she was teaching me. We had come full circle.

## 26

# Circles

Last night I attended the opening performance of the revival of Ben Hecht and Charles MacArthur's **The Front Page,** with a stellar cast that includes Johns Slattery and Goodman, Holland Taylor, Robert Morse, rounded out by the genius of Nathan Lane. The venue was my old stomping ground, the Broadhurst Theatre on Forty-Fourth Street between Broadway and Eighth Avenue. The **New York Times** offices used to be across the street, Sardi's still is, and Times Square is lit up like a Disney spectacular.

Forty years ago, I would walk upstairs from the subway and stop at a deli on Forty-Fourth Street to grab an apple and a turkey-and-avocado sandwich, handed to me by a counterman whose white sleeves were rolled up to the elbows, revealing the tattooed numbers from the concentration camp of his youth. There was not a single piece of bacon in the place. I know this because back then a secretary on lunch break asked for a BLT and the counterman said, "There's not a single piece of bacon in the place."

After getting my LT and coffee, I would make my way across the street to sign in with Bill the door-man (**N.B.: make sure to tip him at the end of the week or he doesn't announce your visitors after the show**). Inside, I walked up the steep gray stairs to my dressing room on the fifth floor, where all the minor players and understudies were stashed, and got ready to deliver my one line—"You look wonderful, sir"—three times. After the performance, it was back on the F train (newly air-conditioned) to my fourth-floor walkup at 108 Dean Street in Brooklyn.

Last night, I stepped out of a hired car and walked the red carpet in front of a crowd of pa-

parazzi. "Over here, Jeffrey!" **Click.** "Up here, Mr. Tambor!" (**Mr. Tambor**—when did that happen?) **Click.** "Hey, Jeff!" **Click.** "Mrs. Tambor, closer to your husband, please!"

I stop to give interviews to live television programs. "We are talking to Jeffrey Tambor live from the Broadhurst Theatre . . ."

I excuse myself for a moment and jog over to the rope line where fans have gathered, to sign a few autographs. Without fans, none of us has a job or a career in show business. "Can we have a selfie with you?" "My girlfriend loves your show." "Could you sign this 'to Amy'?"

I jog back to the carpet for another interview. I hear myself talking, saying more things. I see the interviewer smiling. Whatever I'm saying must be going well. I hear the word "legend." What? No, dial it back. Where's my wife? She's already gone inside. She knows this drill. I'll meet her in our seats.

I hear more words. **Transparent.** Jill Soloway. Changed my life. Revolution.

I can see the stage door right behind the head of the reporter with a mic in his hand, where long ago that man had asked me, "Are you anybody?" He can't be alive. Well, he might be. I'm alive. Now Jon Hamm and Chris Rock are standing there schmoozing. They are standing where I used to grab a smoke after my first scene in Act One.

David Rabe is coming down the red carpet behind me. **That white hair and huge face. Who is**

**that woman on his arm? A date? Of course he has a date. Jill's gone.**

**Concentrate, Jeffrey. Don't evaporate. Stay in this moment.**

"Yes, we're starting Season Four in January."

"Yep, we live in Westchester. Sixteenth anniversary. We married in New Orleans. She waitressed at Birdland, right over there."

I'm leaning against the glass by the door to the lobby. "Here's your ticket, Mr. Tambor. Your wife has gone inside."

I could have sworn the outer lobby was bigger. I got locked in this lobby during the final dress rehearsal of **Sly Fox.** I couldn't get back inside the theater. I scratched and knocked on the glass to snag a passerby. "Would you please go around to the stage door and ask Bill to come and get me?" **Fuck, I'm going to miss my cue. Ah, salvation.** "Thanks, Bill." "Sorry, yeah, they lock on both sides." "Got it."

They are selling headsets for the hearing-impaired inside. Down to the lower lobby to pee before the five-thirty curtain. It's early on opening nights so reviewers can file their reviews and they can be read over the phone at Sardi's across the street at ten-thirty when the first edition comes out.

We ran our lines in a speed-read the day of the **Sly Fox** opening—do it as rapidly as you can, all speed, no acting. Arthur Penn, George C., Héctor, Jack, John, Bob, Trish, Gretchen, me. "You look wonderful, sir"—three times.

An usher escorts me to my seat. D4, the one that's inset from the aisle. That's where I sat to watch rehearsals when we moved from the rehearsal room to the actual theater. Over there, Arthur. Back there, Larry Gelbart. Over there, Gerald Schoenfeld from the Shubert Organization.

Lights to half. "Ladies and gentlemen, please turn off your cell phones." No such announcements back then. The only announcements were to advise of an understudy in the performance.

Curtain up.

**I did a series with that guy over on the right, whatshisname? Chris. . . . Chris McDonald—he and . . . right! Cathy Moriarty—the entire episode took place in a car . . . Oh, did we laugh!**

I used to put my legs over the seat in front of me while I watched rehearsals. Steve, the assistant stage manager, would give me a look.

**The actors are so loud. It's theater, that's how you speak in theater.** That's what Joe Mantello kept telling me in **Glengarry Glen Ross**—"Speak up, this isn't film." **Jesus,** The Front Page, **it's like David Mamet at warp speed.**

**Where's Rabe? What's he thinking? He thanked me for saying hello. Jesus, Jeffrey, he's allowed to date. I wonder if they are more than that. Concentrate. Stay in the moment.**

The actors' attack on the material is astounding. **How did they learn this? They must run it every night. How do they do two performances on**

**matinee days?** They are sweating. I had two shirts, one for Act One, another for Act Two. I would sweat right through my costume, and Josephine the wardrobe supervisor would iron it dry for the evening show. The night I knocked over George C.'s midgame chess set in his dressing room when he was onstage, and Joel Simon (3rd Policeman) remembered the board and put it back in perfect order. Lifesaving.

D4 off the aisle. **Keep your legs down. Learn Héctor's lines. You may have to go on for him someday.**

At the airport, baby boomers give me a Hank Kingsley "Hey now!" Gen Y-ers offer a George Bluth "There's always money in the banana stand." Or the ubiquitous "No touching." At the local Dunkin' Donuts, teenagers call me "Mr. Tambor" and talk about **Transparent.** Little kids ask, "Are you Mr. Salomone from the Plaza Hotel in **Eloise**?" I say, "Yes, I am," and give them a bow.

Watching a trailer for **Trolls,** my kids' faces light up when my voice as King Peppy booms through the theater.

"Daddy, that's you?"

**Are you anybody?**

That's who I am.

# ACKNOWLEDGMENTS

I momentarily lost my mind at the 2016 Emmy Awards. Millions of people witnessed me forget to thank my wife. But as I've said many times before that night and will continue to say until my last breath, I would not have been on that stage, or any stage, or be alive at all without her. My wife, Kasia, came here from Chelm, Poland, when she was seven years old. She grew up "hard" under Communism there, and then in Greenpoint, Brooklyn. She arrived speaking no English, but she educated herself, went to college, and as I write this is on the verge of obtaining her master's while raising four young children. Her first name is Katarzyna, and sometimes I have fun when I answer the phone and someone from the kids' school or the pharmacy wants to speak to her. There is always this pause of horror before they begin, "Is Ka . . . Ka . . ." and then a jumble of sound that sounds like gargling. I admit, I get a kick out of listening to them fall down the rabbit hole. Anyway, people sometimes say to Kasia that they envy her being around so much laughter and glamour and joy, but that's not what it's like to live with me. Kasia is smart, she is a problem solver, and she has an exquisite bullshit detector. She is simply brilliant at life. She will always be that girl who came to visit me on the set with a sandwich in a paper bag. The innocence of it wrecks me still. Thank you, Kasia, for everything. Everything.

# PHOTOGRAPHY CREDITS

Page 26: "UCB Presents ASSSSCAT" (l–r) Matt Besser, Jeffrey Tambor, Jon Gabrus, Tim Meadows, Nicole Byer, Chris Gethard, Adam Pally, Joe Wengert (Brazos Hall, Sunday, March 9, 2014), © Mindy Tucker; page 49: Courtesy of Amazon Content Services LLC; page 51: Courtesy of Amazon Content Services LLC; page 52: **Flea in Her Ear,** courtesy of Joseph Kovoriak/Wayne State University Maggie Allesee Department of Theater and Dance; page 65: **Tartuffe,** © David S. Talbott/courtesy of Jeff Rodgers and the Actors Theatre of Louisville; page 74: **Sly Fox,** © Joseph Abeles/courtesy of the Shubert Archive; page 83: Courtesy of the author; page 147: **And Justice For All** © 1979 Columbia Pictures Industries, Inc. All rights reserved. Courtesy of Columbia Pictures; page 182: Courtesy of Amazon Content Services LLC; page 192: © Jay Thompson, courtesy of Craig Schwartz; page 229: **The Larry Sanders Show,** courtesy of Sony Pictures Television; page 232: **The Larry Sanders Show,** courtesy of Sony Pictures Television; page 234: **The Larry Sanders Show,** courtesy of Sony Pictures Television; page 242: **Arrested Development** © 2004 Twentieth Century Fox Television. All rights reserved.; page 244: **Arrested Development** © 2004 Twentieth Century Fox Television. All rights reserved.; page 246: **Arrested Development** © 2004 Twentieth Century Fox Television. All rights reserved.; page 247: **Arrested Development** © 2004 Twentieth Cen-

ABOUT THE AUTHOR

Jeffrey Tambor is an accomplished actor known for his unforgettable comedic roles on HBO's **The Larry Sanders Show,** the long-running Fox series **Arrested Development,** and the Golden Globe Award–winning **Transparent,** for which he has won Golden Globe and Emmy Awards. Tambor lives in New York.

Ben Barnes is a filmmaker and illustrator who lives in Los Angeles with his pregnant girlfriend, Nicole, and his dog, Ethel Rose. He met Jeffrey at South by Southwest in 2008 and they've gotten along swimmingly ever since.